Parenting
on the Go

Parenting
on the Go

Effective Discipline Strategies
for the Busy, Devoted Parent

by L. Tobin

 Whole Person Associates
Duluth, Minnesota

Whole Person Associates, Inc.
210 West Michigan
Duluth, MN 55802-1908   218-727-0500
E-mail: books@wholeperson.com
Web site: http://www.wholeperson.com

Printed in the United States of America

10 9 8 7 6 5 4 3 2 1

Editorial Director: Susan Gustafson
Art Director: Joy Dey

Library of Congress Catologing in Publication Data 99-69889

ISBN 1-57025-206-8

Helpful books and audio kits from L. Tobin

What Do You Do with a Child Like This?
Journey inside the world of troubled children and learn why they behave as they do. Then create positive change in children's lives with innovative techniques that address their needs.

62 Ways to Create Change in the Lives of Troubled Children
Each page of this flip book offers creative approaches for handling misbehavior and an affirming quote to help build children's self-esteem.

6 Essentials of Discipline
This three-tape audiokit teaches the six skills essential for reducing behavioral difficulties in the home from early childhood through adolescence.

Sticks & Stones & Words Break Bones
The Six Essential Skills in Talking to Angry People so Angry People Will Listen
This two-tape audiokit presents essential anger management instruction for parents, teens, couples, and organizations.

Table of Contents

Introduction

Every day you face innumerable demands upon your time: work, commuting, school, shopping, social commitments—all important, all a priority.

That's true until you become a parent.

Once you have children, all those demands upon your time become much less important. Instead of stealing a few hours from work for an appointment with your hair stylist, you use your third sick day to stay home with an ailing child in a house with empty cupboards because you've not had time to go shopping, and come to think of it, you might not get to the grocery story because the car's nearly out of gas.

At moments such as this, you realize parenting means you'll always be always on the run as you try frantically to be a devoted parent without having the rest of your world—work, marriage, household, health, sanity—fall apart around you. It's not easy.

Then, to make matters worse, in a moment of desperation you locate and purchase a great parenting book only to realize you can't even imagine having the time to read it! If this scenario sounds familiar, hold on. There may be hope yet. Because this book was written for parents just like you—busy, devoted parents who just need a quick idea to get through a difficult moment.

Parenting on The Go is not designed to be read straight through like a traditional book. Instead, it is packaged as a series of three-minute reads, a collection of readily accessible parenting tips that will give you the boost or tip you need to meet the next challenge your child presents then continue on your way.

Each of the eight chapters contains six to ten essential skills in various areas of parenting. Any one of the tips may be exactly what you need to learn at a specific moment—just what you need to pick up the pieces after today's crisis and get going again. And the next day, it's right there waiting for you again with another idea.

So the next time you're at your wits end or wishing you had someone to offer a quick suggestion, open to the table of contents; select the section that seems to best describe your concern; go directly to any item in that section; and give it a try. Got time for another idea? Keep on reading. Or set the book aside for a later look.

That's *Parenting on The Go.* Like a quick e-mail, you get the insight, then get back to what you need to be doing, only now you'll be doing it better.

We hope you'll enjoy the material available to you in this book. For those moments when you can manage as much as fifteen minutes of listening time, perhaps while in the car, we also recommend the author's audiotape series, *Six Essentials of Discipline.* It is a comprehensive presentation of the changing discipline styles you will need as your child progresses from early childhood through the elementary years and into adolescence.

Whether you are reading *Parenting on The Go* or listening to the *Six Essentials of Discipline* audiokits, you'll find in these materials the skills and insights you seek in a capsule form specially designed for you—the devoted parent on the go.

Creating a Disciplined Environment

By designing your home to promote positive behavior, you can prevent many problems before they begin. Here are simple changes that can reduce temptation, help children better organize their time, and help you create understandable rules and routines to make your home run more smoothly.

Create a change
that makes success more likely

Every home has certain tasks that need to be done but which rarely end up being done on time and correctly. In your home it may be cleaning up the toy area or keeping the entryway clear of muddy boots or getting dirty clothes off the bedroom floors and into the laundry room. Whatever it is, you need your kids to do something that they're not doing. Day after day, it's a battle—a battle you don't want to be fighting next week and next month and next year.

Imagine for a moment that in one week your boss is coming to visit. Imagine, too, that your job somehow depends on this particular problem disappearing before she arrives. You like your job and want to keep it, so you can't just hope your kids will miraculously "get it" on their own by then. What could you do to make the change you want more likely to happen? Remember, you are the one who most wants this change.

Consider the changes you could make

Toys are more likely to be put away if you have small boxes for markers, tubes for artwork, and shelves for blocks. You could give up the lowest bookshelf in the living room and make it available for the toys that never seem to make it back to the bedroom. These changes would make picking up toys more likely.

In the entryway, how about placing a box for dirty shoes and a small shelf where homework can be put when the kids arrive home and where completed homework can be found easily as they rush off to school the next morning. Dirty clothes are more likely to be placed in a bedroom hamper than taken to the laundry room daily. And what about some extra hooks on the back of the closet door for hanging clothes that will be worn again? These are changes you could make in a couple minutes.

A change in the timing of what you are asking for might also work. Are clothes more likely to be picked up at night rather than the morning? Do dishes need to be done right after the meal? If getting a chore done is an ongoing problem, would it be more likely to be done if you asked for it at a different time? This, too, is a change you can make.

If you want something to change, you have to be willing to change something. Simple one-minute organizational changes like these can go a long way toward making what you need more likely to happen. You still require your child to do the work—to do what needs to be done—while you take the opportunity to teach the value of planning and organization. Everyone wins and your home runs more smoothly.

Demonstrate one more time

If cleanup never takes place the way you would like it to, it may be that you need to demonstrate one more time exactly what you have in mind. Children who *won't* do what you ask are often kids who *can't*—kids who forget easily and need to see the task done properly one more time. At least it's worth a try.

For example, do the dishes once more, your son working with you, talking aloud through the steps you take along the way.

"For me it works best to put the pots over here so I remember them."

As you walk through an activity, consider the difficulties children have that you don't have—shelves they can't reach, toys that don't fit back in their boxes, drawers that stick.

While cleaning up the garage together with a ten-year-old daughter, point out again the reason why tools need to be kept out of the reach of younger siblings. Explain the reasons behind your organization and precautions; they may not be as obvious as you assumed.

"I keep this electric pruner unplugged because your younger brother is fascinated with it, and it could rip his arm off."

Point out steps that are difficult for you to remember:

"For some reason, it is really hard for me to remember to lock the tool cabinet before I leave. How about for you?"

Acknowledging your difficulty in remembering will ensure your daughter will go out of her way to remember.

You could make a list of cleanup procedures together or you could post written reminders of easy-to-forget items. To help younger children with cleanup, take a photo of the toy shelf or work bench with everything in its place. Tape the photo to the shelf to show exactly what "picked-up" means.

Finally, ask yourself: if I were this child being asked to complete this task, what would I find difficult? What have I not seen my child do right for a long time or ever? Then make the time to demonstrate once again, even if it is for the hundredth time. This time he may finally get it.

Create order from chaos in your home

Stop and think of the area or activity in your home where problems occur most frequently:

_____

_____

Now, without getting stuck thinking that your child should be able to do the task just as it is, what organizational change could you make so what you want is more likely to happen?

_____

_____

_____

If you are having difficulty thinking of something you could do, imagine that you are your child. What change would make it easier for you to remember to do the task and to do it right?

_____

_____

Now, when can you find time to make this change?

_____

_____

You've been spending a lot of time each day fighting this recurring problem. Taking the small amount of time necessary to make this change could end up making a big difference in your day and your child's day. Give it a try.

Manage temptation

You can't remove all the temptations in your home. That would be nice but it's not very practical. However, anyone who has successfully quit smoking or lost weight knows the value of keeping temptation at a manageable level.

In a home where discipline rules, temptation is managed within the limitations of a child—not as we would like children to be, but as we know them to be—ever-curious, relentless explorers of anything within reach.

Reduce misbehavior by reducing temptation
To reduce misbehavior, take at look at the temptations in your home. Imagine yourself as a child. Look around your home. What do you see?

Are kids constantly playing with tantalizing adult possessions? Label areas that are off limits and items that are personal, not family, possessions. This will help. But also assume unlimited curiosity, since that is what being a kid is all about. Accept that anything within your child's reach will be explored.

Remove fragile objects to your own bedroom. Or lock them in a closet or garage. Or store them elsewhere until the kids are older—that is if you really want them to survive your child's early years intact. If tempting objects can't be removed, place them out of reach on upper shelves or cabinets and devote lower shelves and drawers throughout the house to kids' things. In this way, children will feel a sense of belonging throughout the house and not imagine some cabinets as "enemy territory" awaiting the opportunity to be infiltrated.

If guns are in your home, are your precautions adequate? Are the guns locked up? Do kids know where the ammunition is? You may trust your kids to never touch the guns, but are you equally sure you can you trust their friends?

Take a walk through your house, looking not just for safety hazards but also for temptations that are simply not worth the tension they create.

Is junk food a ongoing battle?

Begin by having a healthy snack available when kids arrive home after school. That's when kids are hungry. If conflict continues, could you make available only a one-day supply of treats or make it a point purchase only acceptable between-meal snacks—crackers, for example, rather than potato chips?

To reduce the snack temptation, set aside in the refrigerator snacks that your children can have as soon as they get home from school or at anytime throughout the day. Fruit is always good, as well as vegetables, whole grain crackers, peanut butter, and celery with cream cheese. Post a list of acceptable snacks on the refrigerator door.

Consider a late-afternoon "get-by" snack when your kids are first home and a light meal later in the evening. It's actually more healthful to have a large breakfast and go easy on the evening meal, especially if your family struggles with weight problems and lacks physical activities in the evening. The saying is "eat like a king in the morning and a pauper in the evening."

Or if you eat early in the evening, consider getting the family back together an hour or two after dinner. Eating a light dessert or snack at 8:30 gives the family a chance to gather again, and the children won't be sneaking snacks all evening.

Television, a constant temptation

Are your children learning from TV behaviors you want them to learn? They are learning as they watch as surely as they learn from the behavior of everyone around them. You don't invite angry, aggressive, vulgar people into your home, in part because of their influence on your children. But children can be affected equally if people with those behaviors enter through your television screen.

Limiting TV viewing is not as difficult as you might imagine. Most children will protest at first but will rapidly return to long-neglected activities. Many will even feel relieved as the compulsion to spend hour after hour in front of the TV disappears. Expect an adjustment period, but the return to activities the family can share will be well worth it.

Many books suggest activities that can replace TV viewing and are worth checking out at a local bookstore or library.

Television provides a serious temptation. If you choose not to eliminate it, ongoing efforts to reduce its effects on your children are still worthwhile.

Reduce the temptations in your home

List the temptations your children succumbed to during the past week:

_____

_____

_____

_____

_____

Consider those temptations one at a time. What changes could you make that would reduce the level of temptation and thus reduce the misbehavior?

_____

_____

_____

_____

It's not wise to make a lot of changes all at once. With which one or two will you begin?

_____

_____

_____

Create creatures of habit

The hardest way to establish order in your home is with words.

"Put your clothes away right now, wash your face, your room is a mess, clean it up immediately."

If that is what you find yourself saying all day long, it's time to rely instead on routines.

Think of routines not so much as rules, but rather as procedures— procedures that help the house run more smoothly and keep you from sounding like you're making up new rules every day.

"Teeth are brushed before the story begins."

"Homework starts right after dinner, then TV if there is time."

Routines help children by providing cues that point to what needs to be done next without you reminding them. Routines will go a long way toward helping your home run more smoothly

Routines help with recurring activities

So you won't have to negotiate each time, establish routines for recurring activities. What routines would you like to have in your home regarding meals, bedtime, television, homework, chores, and special events, such as sleep-overs? To provide built-in reminders, tie the routines to other activities or to the natural rhythms of the day.

"Check to see that the bedroom window is relocked each morning before you come downstairs for breakfast."

"Saturday chores are done before you leave the house."

"Before you walk in the house after school, always check to see that the back door is secure."

When routines involve time, be sure to give children more time than you might expect will be needed. When you rush children, they may feel that you disapprove of or are indifferent to their efforts.

"The kitchen timer goes off fifteen minutes before the bus arrives. That's enough time to brush your teeth and be ready."

Establishing routines not only reduces arguments but more important provides security and predictability to children's lives.

Build new routines

Building a routine is easiest if it involves some concrete action on your part:

"Here is an alarm clock for you to use."

"I've written out the times you can use the phone so you can tell your friends."

Tying your child's routine to an activity of your own can also help:

"As soon as you hear my hair dryer shut off, that's the time for you to come in and brush your teeth so we can leave on time."

Or do it together:

"Time for us to brush."

When first establishing a new routine, give ample advance warning:

"Five more minutes before it's time to get dressed."

But later, it's a good idea to remind with as few words as possible:

"Five minutes."

To avoid arguments, discuss the need for the routine and write it down where children can easily see it. Children may not like routines at first, but neither do they like constant reminders. Explain that routines reduce the need for reminders, and they will get the idea.

When you establish a routine, you can include a discussion about when the routine might change as your child matures and assumes additional responsibility:

"When you turn seven, that's when we will discuss a later bedtime for you."

With older kids, you can agree to negotiate with grace but not at the moment:

"I'd be happy to discuss a later bedtime with you. We can do that on Saturday morning before chore time. Now it is time for bed."

Stick to routines but be flexible

Rigid routines: "It's just too bad they scheduled the first Mars landing at 5:30 because you know we eat at that time!" ensure frustration and anger. Routines are to help the house run more smoothly not just to tie everyone to a whole new set of rules. You might even discuss before-hand special circumstances in which routines will change, such as when friends or relatives visit:

"Yes, it is chore time, Sara, but you can wait to sweep under the chair until after your grandmother leaves."

Routines provide a great opportunity to teach both the value of order and the importance of flexibility.

Establish order through routines in your home.

Recall one regular battle that involves a disagreement over how or when something should be done.

_____

_____

Is your child old enough to participate in helping you establish a routine? If not, what routine could you impose that would serve both your interests and your child's interests—a routine that makes sense and stands a chance of lasting more than a day or two?

_____

_____

To help your child remember, can you tie this routine to something new that you can initiate or to an activity you do regularly or to a natural reminder in your home?

_____

_____

Under what circumstances would you need to be flexible?

_____

_____

When might you be willing to renegotiate this routine?

_____

_____

Routines serve primarily to reduce the need for you to be constantly reminding your child. A good routine should serve both of you. Remember that you can establish order through routines more easily than you can rule with words.

Family business

Is there time in your home to discuss family business? A time to gather and talk about problems, plans, and changes that might make the family run more smoothly?

In some homes this takes place routinely during meals or before bedtime. In other homes, it never happens.

Setting aside a special time once a week, or even as little as once a month, to discuss rules, chores, what's working and what isn't working in your home can reduce the chance that the same problems will continue month after month.

Include young children

You can invite children into family discussions when they are very young, showing them that their opinions are listened to and valued even if their suggestions aren't always followed. Asking children to participate in family discussions gives them a sense of being responsible to the family not just a responsibility of the family.

Family discussion time doesn't need to be anything more than a regular opportunity to talk together about things that concern all of you. It could be a formal sit-down meeting in the living room at a set time to review an agenda developed through the week on a page posted where everyone can record the issues they want discussed during the next meeting.

But discussions don't need to look like formal meetings. Any regular activity can serve as a time to talk. Just begin the tradition of discussing family concerns at a regular time. Soon, it will be expected and anticipated. Here's how a few families have made it work:

"We try to all be together for dinner Thursday night so we can discuss our plans for the weekend."

"We walk to the store Saturday morning. That relaxed atmosphere provides a good time to talk about problems."

"It works well for us to meet over an evening snack on Sunday night."

Children look to you to set the tone for family time, to talk about things that aren't discussed otherwise:

"We'll talk about bathroom schedules Friday night at 6:30 when there is nothing on TV that anyone wants to watch."

Family meetings involve children in the process of being a family. They give you an opportunity to teach the skills of group decision making, to help children listen to each other, and to work together to arrive at solutions.

Family discussion times are ideal for dealing with sibling difficulties with everyone in the family available to suggest solutions to questions such as:

"How are you and your sister getting along when you walk to school together?"

During these discussions, you teach your children how to discuss conflicts and resolve disagreements at a quiet time rather than during the heat of an argument.

Time alone with each child is important, too

Family time is important, but individual time for each child is equally important in preventing misbehavior. This may be no more than a few minutes during a regular activity, even washing dishes, that is done with one child alone and (preferably) just one parent. The important thing is that each child knows there will be one time each day or week when they don't have to compete with siblings or the other parent for attention.

During individual time, all attention goes to the child—discussing the child's concerns or simply sharing a child-selected activity together.

It doesn't need to be a long time. Even five or ten minutes is fine if it's regular:

"Dad will play with you for a few minutes while I begin supper. You decide what to play."

Planning for family time and for individual time with each child will help eliminate problems before they occur. Both take time you may not think you have, but if they reduce the time you now spend dealing with misbehavior and negative ways of getting your attention, they will be well worth the effort.

Schedule family discussions in your home

To ensure children know they are important to the family, involve them in discussions of family matters.

Are there special times that already exist in your family, times when important things are discussed? It may be that you already have a family meeting tradition.

_____

_____

If not, when does the family tend to be together?

_____

_____

What is one piece of family business that you would like to discuss with every member at a time with no interruptions?

_____

_____

_____

Which child do you feel most needs special time with you?

_____

What is the child already doing that you could join in with all of your attention, or what new activity would you enjoy together?

_____

_____

These changes may seem to require time that you don't have. But the benefits will be evident very soon. Could you begin this week?

_____

By scheduling time together, you can deal with family and individual concerns before they become problems.

Rules and reasons

No one really enjoys rules. But fortunately most children understand the need for rules. They can be taught to understand rules that keep them safe and rules that respect the rights of others in the family.

Children need to learn to create rules not just follow them

Involving your kids in the creation of family rules is the best way to end up with rules that work—rules that last more than a day or two.

The best time to design rules is not in the heat of conflict. To develop a rule to handle a recurring problem, set up a time to discuss it when calm thinking is possible. Any rule will work best if it is explained, specific, and valued.

Explain first why a rule is needed. Even very young children can understand how rules are needed for safety or to reduce conflict in a family. But try to explain the reason you feel it is needed, even if your child fails to agree with you:

"I don't feel it is safe for you at ten years old to be outside late in the evening. We need to come up with a reasonable time for you to be home to ensure your safety and my peace of mind."

If the rule is negotiable, discuss it. If it is not negotiable, don't invite discussion.

Second, be specific and anticipate difficulties:

"6:30 is all right. But you need to be inside before 6:30. If you have a problem getting home by that time, I expect a call."

Then add a reason for your child to want to comply:

"When you get in at 6:30, we can sit down together and work on that new computer program. If you come home earlier, we can get started sooner."

By explaining the need for a rule, inviting specific suggestions, and providing a reason for the child to comply, children can come to understand the need for and the benefits of rules in a family.

Involve your children in rule making

Think of one rule you wish you had established long ago in your home, a rule needed for safety or to avoid conflict:

_____

_____

Are you willing to invite suggestions, or is what you need done clear, specific and nonnegotiable?

_____

_____

When would your child be most open to understanding, most willing to recognize the importance of the rule?

_____

_____

To prepare yourself, write the reason why this rule is needed:

_____

_____

Describe specifically what is to be done:

_____

_____

Is there anything you could add as an additional enticement?

_____

_____

Finally, is there a time when this rule will no longer be needed or when you would be willing to renegotiate with your child? Can you give your child any hope of greater responsibility at a later time?

_____

_____

Anticipate disagreement

No matter how fair the rules and how well established the routines in your home, it is still your child's job to try to negotiate more privileges. It is your child's responsibility to continually inform the world that each month she is older and is capable of new freedoms and responsibilities. So, accepting that challenging you is your child's job, be prepared with a couple of set answers.

When the rule is not negotiable, show that it and what your child says can exist side by side. Do this by simply repeating what your child says, linking it to the rule with the word "and."

"Yes, you are very responsible for your age, and three-year-olds do not cross the street alone.

"I know you would both go to sleep early, and sleep-overs are allowed only on the weekends."

When the argument comes and you are willing to negotiate, tie what your child wants to what will make it work for you. Use the words "after" or "as soon as" or "once you."

"I'll read you a second story after you brush your teeth and have your pajamas on."

"I'm willing to extend curfew a half hour once you complete all your homework."

Prepare for expected challenges with these two pat answers: repeating your child's words and restating the rule, or agreeing to renegotiate "as soon as" or "after" you get what you need. Using pat answers buys you time to manage your anger and not be overly upset with a child who is acting exactly like a child, wanting more responsibility every day.

Prepare for disagreement by practicing set replies.

The nonnegotiable rule: No stuffed toys outside.

The argument: "I'll keep them on the grass."

Standing your ground: "Yes I know you'd keep them on the grass, and no stuffed toys outside."

The nonnegotiable rule: No dates on school nights.

The argument: "We'd do our homework together."

Staying your ground: "Yes I believe you would do your homework, and no dates on school nights."

Or, with a willingness to negotiate:

"You can take out your stuffed toys when you first bring out a blanket so the toys will stay clean."

"You can go out on a date tonight, provided you both complete your homework here at the house first."

Practice anticipating disagreements

Think of an argument you are likely to get in response to a rule you have in place:

What is the rule? _____

_____

What is the argument? _____

_____

Now repeat the argument, add the word "and," and restate the rule.

_____

_____

This time agree to what is being asked, stating the condition under which it will be acceptable to you:

Yes, you can _____

as soon as _____

Increasing Communication

The techniques presented in this section will help you communicate better with your child, especially during difficult times. Learn to describe problems rather than assign blame, to speak first from positive assumptions, and to use words to resolve rather than escalate problems.

Reframe struggles as emerging strengths

Everyone has something to learn. Even at your age, you may still be struggling with the best way to deal with anger or loneliness or boredom. Those challenges, once overcome, can even become strengths.

In the same way, personality traits in your children that lead to misbehavior at this time may later become their greatest strengths.

Is your child assertive—lets you know exactly what he thinks? As a lawyer, that will be an asset. Is she self-motivated—the group goes one way, she the other? That is a trait shared by millionaire entrepreneurs. Is he energetic—overflowing with vitality? Independent—confidently wandering away? Determined—unswerving in what he wants? Social—always talking? Creative—you can't anticipate what she will come up with next? When your children become adults you will want them to be assertive, self-motivated, energetic, independent, determined, social, and creative. At the moment, however, they need your help to learn to use these qualities in a positive rather than a negative way.

Help your children believe in their future
You can help your children believe in their future by describing their struggles in a positive rather than a negative way.

"You're very sensitive to criticism, and that is getting you in trouble with this teacher. But being sensitive is a good quality. Let's talk about how you can be both sensitive and able to receive criticism."

By describing your child's personality with a positive term "sensitive" rather than with a negative term "oversensitive" or worse yet with "You're a baby," you can point out what she needs to learn—how to accept criticism—but without being insulting.

"It's good to be assertive. But telling the principal that you think he's stupid is going to get you in a lot of trouble. How could you tell him exactly what you were upset about?"

Going out of your way to use positive descriptions also helps you to see the child in a positive light, even during difficult times.

"Yes, he is adventurous. I hope you find him soon, officer."

Giving positive descriptions to challenging behaviors keeps you focused on what specifically you can teach your child in order for that quality to become a strength later in life. And your child stays positive about who he is along the way.

Identify the future strength that underlies current misbehavior

Consider assertiveness. Can a child who screams at you when upset be considered a child who is very assertive? Sure, and later in life that assertiveness will serve her well. But she will need to learn to express her discontent in ways that make people want to listen. Tell her:

"I'm glad you let people know when you're upset; it's good to be assertive like that. But your screaming doesn't make me want to listen to you. If, instead of screaming at me, you tell me, 'I'm upset and need to talk to you right now,' I will stop and listen to what you have to say."

Consider independence. A child who continually runs away can be considered to be very independent. And that is a good quality in life. But he will need to learn how to explore safely.

"You're independent, an explorer, and that's good. But there is a difference between being brave and being foolish that every explorer has to learn. Your challenge is to be brave and wise. Let's talk about why I'm afraid when I turn around in the store and I can't find you."

Seeing through to the positive quality is not always easy. Sometimes it helps to imagine the child being the opposite of what he is. Would you want a child who never speaks up for himself? Or a child who is afraid to be alone?

Using positive description isn't a ploy to cover up your child's faults;

it is simply a way to focus on what the child needs to learn to be better at being himself.

Put a positive spin on your child's behavior

If you were to describe your child's behavior in a negative way, what would you call it?

_____

_____

From your child's perspective, how could you describe that same behavior in a positive way. If you were your child you might see yourself as very . . .

_____

_____

If you are having difficulty, imagine your child later in life using this same quality in a way that ends up making him very successful. How might you describe this same quality in a successful adult?

_____

_____

Now describe this to your child. "You are a very . . ."

_____

What does the child need to learn to turn this ability in a positive direction? Be as specific as possible, "though you'll need to learn to . . ."

_____

Keep this positive description in mind when you are describing your child to neighbors or relatives, reminding them how to stay positive about your child as well.

Forewarn by stating what *to* do

Do you often hear yourself using the word "don't" to warn children about what not to do in the future? Are there times when you seem to use it almost continuously?

"Don't walk in that mud puddle."

"Don't drop that dirty towel on the floor."

"Don't" is a word most parents use often, though commonly with a feeling of "Why did I bother?" You see, "don't" sentences are not very effective communication. Any sentence that begins with the word "don't" goes on to describe, often in great detail, exactly what you don't want to take place—what the child is not to do—but it fails to tell the child what to do. With only a little more thought, you can instead describe exactly what to do: "Stay on the sidewalk," or "Drop the towel in the hamper as you walk by." Using positive directions in this way will be far more effective in bringing about the behavior you want to see.

"Don't" sentences are often rather insulting

"Don't drop that dirty towel on the floor," assumes your child intends to do the wrong thing. You appear to be yelling at him in advance. Your child is likely to feel the way you do when your boss tells you, "Don't forget what I told you yesterday."

Instead of starting your sentence with "don't," try instead, "I know" or "you know."

"You know to stay on the sidewalk away from the puddle."

"I know you will drop that towel in the hamper as you walk by."

When your child reaches for a full glass of orange juice, it's tempting to caution, "Don't spill that glass of juice on the floor." Try instead, "I know you will hold that glass with both hands." The statement must be made in a matter-of-fact manner, without sarcasm. If your child's response is, "I know" or "I will" that's fine. Maybe you won't have to say anything at all next time. But at least you are leading with faith in your child's abilities rather than doubt.

Here's a statement parents make over and over: "Don't take that toy away from your brother." Try instead, "I know you will ask your brother for the toy," or "You know to ask if you want something your brother is playing with."

Affirmating statements bring your child's awareness to something just as a "don't" sentence does, but they provide positive rather than negative reminders. Communication with your child will be far more effective if you avoid the word "don't" and instead describe what you want, reminding with "I know" or "You know to."

When danger threatens

Describing what you want the child *to* do rather than what you don't want is essential when your child is in danger. If your child is on the sill of an open window, rather than saying, "Don't turn around and look down or you'll fall," describe instead exactly want you want him to do. "Feet down," or "Come to me," are two positive statements that plant in your child's mind exactly what he should do to save his life.

If your child were to find a gun in the bushes at a park, rather than yelling, "Don't touch the trigger," thus directing his thoughts to the point of danger, it would be better to say:

"Freeze."

"Point the gun at the ground."

"Set the gun down now."

Direct his thoughts to anything but the trigger.

Practice making positive statements and affirmations

Getting away from the word "don't" will take practice. But each time you describe what you want or lead with faith rather than doubt, it will feel better to you than the "don't" sentence you have already used a thousand times.

Think of a "don't" sentence you are likely to use today:

_____

_____

Now think of exactly what you want your child *to* do. This may be difficult at first, but it will become easier with practice. Try it:

_____

_____

"Don't yell," becomes "Speak in a voice I will listen to."

"Don't hit your sister," becomes "Tell your sister what you are upset about."

"Don't be obnoxious," becomes "Tell me exactly what you want and I will tell you when I will have time to help you with it."

Now think of another "don't" sentence you will likely use today to remind your child of what she should or should not do. Think of something you remind her of almost every day:

_____

_____

Now state it as an affirmation beginning with "I know" or "You know:

_____

_____

"Don't forget your homework again this morning," becomes "I know you will remember your homework as you walk out the door," or "You know you have homework to return, right."

Avoid "don't" sentences by using positive directions and affirmations to set a more positive tone to your daily communication with your child.

Remind with cues and few words

The most common complaint made by parents is that their children don't listen. Does this sound familiar?

"You left the door open again. How many times have I told you to close it. Can't you remember a simple thing like this?"

The fact is, if you have told your children a thousand times to not slam the door, they probably do not need to have it explained again—but they may still need to be reminded. And that is done best with as few words as possible, "Screen door."

To get children to listen to you more, you might begin by talking less
One-word cues remind without repetitive and demeaning explanations. "Screen door" can convey all that needs to be said about a slammed door.

Lectures are usually boring and condescending. Hasty threats are often silly and impossible to follow through on. And endless scolding and criticism provides little incentive for the child to change.

More often than not a reminder is all that is needed anyway: "Homework before dinner." "Quiet time."

By simply stating without anger or condescension what needs to be done at this moment (as if you were a Broadway director giving a cue to an actor), you can remind without the buildup of emotion that usually accompanies more words. Say or do the least possible to get your child back on track again—one finger might be enough—pointing to the door if it's time to leave or pantomiming brushing teeth as a reminder that it's time to brush.

Sudden silence can also get attention. Or consider a comical pantomime to remind and break the tension. Or demonstrate what needs to be done in an extra-slow or exaggerated manner. Any action that gets the point across without long-winded, verbal explanations will remind children of the innumerable little things that adults give importance to—actions like closing doors—that will never be a priority for a five-year-old.

Use as few words as possible to correct behavior

If your child needs to learn (or unlearn) social behaviors, you can contract with her to do what is needed when you supply a visual reminder. If, for example, your child has a poor sense of personal space, standing uncomfortable close to other children and splattering them when she speaks, she may be unaware of other people's discomfort.

First, ask her if she would like to have more friends. Once she agrees that she wants the result, you can introduce the method:

"When you are standing uncomfortably close to someone, I will call your name and touch my cheek with my finger. That will remind you to step back so the person doesn't feel crowded."

Using cues in this way is particularly effective when the child would be embarrassed to have you correct the behavior out loud.

"I'll simply hand you a tissue or point to the tissue box when it is time for you to wipe your nose. If you will blow your nose when I do this, I'll stop telling you again and again in front of your friends. Is that a deal?"

Reducing the words you use to correct a child will increase the child's willingness to do what you ask. Getting your child to listen better begins with using your words more effectively.

Use behavior cues in your home

Think of an action that you constantly remind your child of—something you have told him to do "a thousand times."

Now, what would be a single word you could use to remind your child of this, accepting the idea that she just needs to be reminded.

What nonverbal signal might work as well—a gesture or pantomime? Would it need to be explained to your child or can you just start using it as a way to remind without launching into the same old lecture.

Try it out next time. You'll probably find that your child will appreciate the respect you are showing by making your point without lecturing.

Take time to explore opinions

Raising children requires a lot of listening. Listening well is a skill, one you are probably better at it some times than other times.

You show you are listening to your child when you turn your body directly toward him so he literally "has both your ears." Looking directly at your child lets him know you are not thinking of ten other things while merely pretending to listen.

Listen when you have time and tell your child directly when you don't have time. If you are unable to pay attention at the moment, make plans to talk with him at a specific time. "I have to finish this now, Kyle. In ten minutes I'll be able to listen to your story."

The hard part, of course, is getting back to your child without needing to be asked again.

Show that you are listening

You show you are listening when you acknowledge and clarify your child's feelings. This is more than just parroting back what your child said:
"I hate school."
"Oh you hate school, huh."

Try instead to restate what you think she is feeling in more specific language:

"You sound discouraged with the score you got in math."

Acknowledging feelings can be difficult because we often don't want to accept the fact that our children feel disappointed, angry, sad, afraid, or jealous.

Acknowledge and accept feelings

Too often in the face of difficult emotions, our attempt to quickly fix the feeling only denies or minimizes what the child is feeling:

"No, you don't hate school."

Instead of denying the feeling, let your child know that you have heard what she feels and you care about what she is feeling. Trying to fix the problem by denying the emotion may turn the child's anger toward you for not listening:

"You don't care how I feel."

Instead, explore your child's feelings, teaching the words for emotions without imposing your judgment as to whether she "should' or "should not" feel what she feels:

"You're upset. Can you tell me what happened?"

"What don't you like about school?"

Acknowledging feelings can be particularly difficult when your child expresses those feelings harshly:

"I hate you. You're mean to me."

Harsh words often reflect only the directness of the child's vocabulary and the intensity of her feelings at the moment. Accepting that you will not be liked 100 percent of the time is essential for healthy parenting. In their children's best interests, parents must often do what children don't like. So acknowledge the feelings and restate the rule:

"I know you're angry, and the street is not safe at night."

Later you can talk about not using the word "hate" if that is offensive to you.

Acknowledging feelings lets your child know that you hear what she is feeling, and though you can't fix it, you are on her side. Often, that is all your child needs from you.

If your child says, "I hate my teacher," you could respond: "What exactly are you upset with her about?" or "Sounds like something went wrong today."

If you send your child to bed on time rather than let him watch a late TV program, you can respond to his complaint, "You're mean and I hate you," by saying, "The program is for adults. It wouldn't be good for you. My job is to keep you safe."

Explore and accept your child's feelings

Take the time to explore your child's opinions to learn more about what she feels and thinks.

Recall an opinion your child has that you usually deny—perhaps something she "hates" or finds disgusting:

_____

_____

Now think of two questions you could ask that would give you more information about your child's opinion:

You might begin with

Can you explain _____

or Tell me more about _____

or What do you think _____

The goal is to not tell the child what you think but to draw out more information about what the child thinks. In this way, you can go beyond: "You don't really want to get your teacher fied," into a discussion of the thinking behind the remark.

"What would be the best thing about having a new teacher?"

"What would you want to do differently with a new teacher?"

When your children express opinions, they offer you insight into their thoughts, hopes, and fears—but only if you are willing to listen and not afraid of what you hear. You can learn a lot about your children by taking the time to listen, acknowledging emotions, and exploring opinions whenever they offer them.

Confront negative talk with positive facts

The way children describe themselves can either tie them to the past or lead them to more positive future behavior. If your child describes himself in negative terms, "I'm stupid. I never do anything right," you know it does no good to say, "You are not stupid, and I don't want to hear you say that again."

Instead of giving your opinion, present the facts:

"Last week you finished your work in record time, and it was all correct."

"Remember when you thought you would never learn to ride a bike. And now look at you go."

If the negative self-criticism has a history, mention the change that has occurred:

"You used to strike out a lot, but not any more."

"You used to have trouble in school, but you haven't recently."

Don't let self-defeating remarks go unchallenged

Take a moment to offer the healthier perspective that the child lacks:

"This is difficult at first. Everyone has trouble with it. You'll get it with practice."

"There is a difference between not being able to do something and not having done it before. You're just beginning. It will come."

Saying something like, "Frustrating, huh? Double-digit division is tough at first, everyone struggles with it," goes a long way toward helping a child understand he is not just "dumb, dumb, dumb" but simply up against something difficult.

Confront negative talk, not with just your opinions, but with the facts and perspective your child lacks.

Confront your child's negative self-talk

Negative thinking is not innocent or forgettable. It is powerful and defeating. Ignoring it will make your child believe you agree with it.

Think of one negative or self-defeating comment that you are likely to hear in your home in the near future:

_____

_____

Now, think of an incident or a fact that confronts or contradicts this negative perspective. Record it here just as you would say it to your child:

_____

_____

Have this response ready to use the next time you hear the self-defeating comment. Remember to just state the fact and not necessarily get into an argument with the child over the opinion. State the fact that contradicts your child's negative opinion and then move on.

Teach actions that can change moods

Give your children a powerful tool by teaching them to take control of their moods.

Your children probably know they can talk themselves into a bad mood. But do they know how to talk themselves into feeling better? Children can learn early in life that they can't always control what happens to them but they can control how they think about it and how long they dwell on it.

Sometimes a bad mood requires that your child talk about what she is feeling, but other times, a bad mood simply demonstrates that she hasn't learned tricks that will help her feel more "up" than "down."

Tricks to change moods

To improve a bad mood, make yourself do what you would do if you felt good. Teach this skill to your child by asking what he would be doing if he weren't in a bad mood.

If he responds, "I'd probably be playing outside," encourage him to begin even though he is not in the mood for it. This is important. Simply beginning activities we may not be in the mood for can be the best way to change a mood.

Teach children that another way to trick themselves out of a bad mood is simply to put on a smile and act as if they were happy. Remind them of the thoughts that can bring them out of a bad mood.

If a bad mood comes from negative thinking, give your child a positive thought to repeat to himself and thus take control of what he is thinking.

"I can learn things I never thought I could learn."

"I can overcome my fears."

"I can be fun and a good friend. Kids will like me once they get to know me."

Of course, it is always important to first listen to your child describe being unhappy. But if the conversation seems to be going nowhere, it's time to teach your child to actively adjust his mood.

Help your children understand that feeling bad or sad or frustrated is normal for everyone. Teach them the tricks we all use to get ourselves out of a bad mood. In this way they will grow to understand that being in a bad mood is normal, but it's possible to choose how long they want to stay there. When they are tired of feeling depressed or angry, they can take action to begin feeling better.

Keep a running list of possible mood elevators

Start a list on the wall of "Thoughts When I Am Happy" and "Things I Do When I Feel Good."

It's important that these be written not as things guaranteed to make your child happy—because they won't always—but simply as statements of things she does when she is happy.

When you recognize your child's self-defeating thoughts, record on this list positive self-statements that she can practice if she would like to. If your child feels overwhelmed with schoolwork, the positive affirmation might be, "I can do my best and move forward each day." Or keep a list of things she has now mastered that she once thought she would never learn, "I used to be afraid of water, but now I can swim like a fish."

With a handy list of mood elevators and positive affirmations, your child has a place to go for ideas when she wants to feel better.

Teach your children to help themselves feel more positive

Make a list of your own mood adjusters. Write down the things that you do when you are feeling good, the things you look forward to:

_____

_____

_____

_____

_____

_____

You might want to post this where your children can see it, then let your children watch you refer to the list when you are not feeling at your best.

Write an affirmation for yourself:

_____

_____

By simply watching you adjust your mood, your children will pick up the tips you have learned over the years and begin taking charge of their own moods.

Reward small improvements

Often the hardest thing to do as a parent is to reward or praise children when their behavior is better but is still a long way from what you want it to be.

Imagine that your child has been throwing rocks at people as they walk by. One day you see him toss a rock at your house. Now that isn't what you want either, but it is better than throwing at the neighbors.

If you respond as severely to throwing rocks at the house as you did to throwing rocks at the neighbor, you'll miss the chance to notice and respond to the progress he's made. He isn't doing everything you want, but he's getting there. By noticing his progress, you can help him along the way:

"I'm glad you are no longer throwing at the neighbors. Now let's see if there is something to throw at that isn't freshly painted. How about that tree. Can you hit it with this ball?"

With practice, you can interpret the smallest change as the start of a new beginning:

"All day today without a fight at school. Good job."

"Your mother doesn't like that word much, but I'm glad you didn't say what you said to her last time."

Pointing out very small successes is particularly useful when you are overwhelmed with all the child is doing wrong and can't imagine anything good to say. At times like this, capture the least imaginable improvement and jump on it:

"You've gone five whole minutes without a mean word to your sister. You're getting older."

Imagine even the smallest incident as the start of change:

"You're remembering to ask to get on the swing this week" (though you saw it just once).

Present even the smallest indication of change as a new fact:

"Tell your father that you are remembering to ask for the swing."

Any sign of improvement can be a new beginning. If you acknowledge the change convincingly, it's more likely that it will be.

Be alert for small improvements

You've been struggling for days to stop your child from using the "f" word, now you hear him use the "sh" word. Neither are acceptable to you, but progress has been made. You might acknowledge the improvement by saying:

"It's good you are not using the "f" word. This "sh" word will still get you in trouble in school though. Let's think of another word that won't get you in trouble."

Here's another example. When you go to the grocery store, every five minutes your child asks for a candy bar. This time almost ten minutes have gone by without him asking. You don't want him pestering you for candy in the store at all, but progress has been made. You could call attention to his improved behavior by saying:

"Look at how good you have been about not asking for candy while we are shopping. You've gone ten whole minutes. Let's stop for a treat on the way home, not candy, but something else I promise you'll enjoy."

Pointing out progress, even when it's very small, is the best way to cement that change in the child's mind. State it as fact, and move on.

Recognize first steps in a better direction

Recall something your child does that you would rather he didn't do. Select a problem on which little progress has been made:

_____

_____

Now, what is the smallest amount of improvement you can imagine? State it in terms of better behavior or time without the unacceptable behavior:

_____

_____

Consider how you might acknowledge this improvement to your child. Try not to make too big of deal of it, "Wow, you went two minutes without hitting. I'm sure you will never ever in your life hit another child," but acknowledge the progress, "Two minutes without hitting. You're playing very well today."

What are the words you could say to your child to offer praise for some amount of progress?

_____

_____

When you feel overwhelmed with all that is going wrong, your child probably feels that way, too. With a little imagination, you can always, always find something to believe might be a new beginning. A little imagination and a little praise can go a long way.

Responding Effectively to Misbehavior

Selecting your battles is the key to responding to misbehavior without overreacting or increasing conflict. Learn the importance of describing exactly what you expect. By offering choices and holding your child to understandable consequences, a moment of misbehavior can be the best moment to teach what your child most needs to learn.

Lead with a minimal response

Excessive verbal confrontation is a sign of an inexperienced parent. The experienced parent knows that sometimes the most powerful reprimands involve no words at all. To break a habit of overreacting, always try "the look" before you fly into a verbal tirade. A firm, cold stare may communicate all that needs to be said. Often misbehavior is just an experiment that the child knows is over as soon as he sees your eyes.

A child who ran through the house knocking over a table and all that was on it does not need to be told:

"Look what a mess you've made. Why can't you be more careful? How many times . . . ?"

He does, however, need to know that you saw the incident and that you expect him to pick the table up right away. Often that can be communicated best with just a look.

Highly verbal parents tend to underestimate children's ability to learn without adult explanations and reprimands. But to see a child make a mistake and know that nothing needs to be said can be very powerful for both of you. If a stern look isn't enough, you can go on to more forceful responses. But next time, try the look again to see if it might communicate all that is necessary.

Silence can be memorable

A common error of inexperienced parents is believing that you need to respond verbally to everything a child says to you. You don't.

When you tell a child, "five minutes until your bath," and you know he will eventually comply, you don't need to respond when he says, "I'm not going to take a bath tonight." Walk away, continue to prepare the bath. When it is time, acknowledge what he said and what needs to be done.

"I know you are not excited about taking a bath. And you know tonight is bath night. It's ready now, no discussion, let's go."

Ignoring the comment initially makes a strong statement that you will not be drawn into a discussion of what is not negotiable. Later you can acknowledge what he said, having established first that the bath will take place.

If your child continues to argue or resist, you have a battle on your hands that may require additional discussion, a choice, or a statement of consequences. But often, a firm nonresponse will be more powerful than any argument you might give.

By simply restating what you originally said and then not responding to the child's invitation to argue, you can avoid spending the present fighting about the future.

Try a minimal response

Recall one minor difficulty that often escalates into a major battle:

_____

_____

_____

How do you respond at the first sign of trouble? What are your first words?

_____

_____

If you usually say too much, too soon, determine next time to not say anything new. Giving a confident look, turn directly to the child and restate what needs to take place. Show that you have no doubt that she will do what is asked, and proceed as if no discussion were possible. Write that confident statement:

_____

_____

If your child continues to argue, simply restate what you said the first time:

_____

_____

A minimal response will not, of course, always be enough, but it's a good beginning.

Direct what you expect

If you can describe specifically what you expect a child to do, it is far more likely to be done. Conversely, if you can't even describe it, your child isn't likely to be able to do it.

For example, if you can't describe how your child is to entertain herself for forty-five minutes in the doctor's waiting room, it is difficult to criticize her attempts at self-entertainment—whatever they might be.

Rather than continue a string of, "Don't do this! Don't do that!" take the time to suggest what she could do:

"See how many dogs in that magazine look like dogs you know in the neighborhood."

Only if you can describe good behavior, can you expect it. A lot of misbehavior occurs during times when we expect children to do nothing, times while we do what we need to do—drive to the store, shop, prepare dinner. It's easy to overestimate your child's ability to self-entertain in a positive manner. In fact, your child may be as uncertain of what to do as you are.

Rather than continual reminders of what not to do, misbehaving children need suggestions for activities more entertaining than misbehavior.

"I'll be in the store for ten minutes. Pull out the comics you brought, and I'll be back before you know it. "

Requiring yourself to describe what you want your children to be doing is much more demanding that simply telling them what not to do. You'll have to brainstorm ideas together rather than just expecting your children to "find something else to do." But if you practice this, you will find it an effective deterrent to misbehavior. In response to your positive suggestions, children will often readily redirect themselves into positive alternatives.

Teach kids to entertain themselves

Kids differ greatly in their ability to entertain themselves. If your children spend large amounts of time watching television or videos, they may no longer be very good at entertaining themselves with toys alone.

Consider reducing television time. Limiting television time in your home by even one hour in the evening or one day in the week or, if you are daring, for a whole week will greatly increase your children's ability to entertain themselves. You may be surprised at how well your family will adapt—after the initial moments of dissension. Even the most addicted child will often find it a relief if the television is taken away for a few days. Pull out the activities or games that have been set aside and play together with your kids.

Beyond this, review the entertainment possibilities during difficult times. What is in the car to play with? What could a child bring along to the store when shopping? Brainstorm suggestions for what children can do when their friends come over.

Share ideas with other parents. Ask a teacher for suggestions. What do the kids do at school when given a choice?

When misbehavior occurs, think alternatives first and punishment only later.

Prepare for difficult times

Consider the times in your child's day that misbehavior occurs most frequently. When would that be in your home?

_____

_____

What is one alternative activity that might be more engaging than what they are coming up with on their own?

_____

_____

Is there anything that needs to be supplied beforehand?

_____

_____

If you don't have any ideas, brainstorm together with your child.

Describe the problem and what needs to be done

When you respond to misbehavior with criticism, sarcasm, and blame, your child often stops thinking of what she has done wrong and thinks only of how to defend herself from your wrath.

"I told you to remember to close the door. But no, you have to leave it open time after time. You never listen to me, do you."

While such comments may describe what you are feeling, they distract your child's attention from what she has done and what she needs to do now.

To respond to misbehavior more effectively, keep your comments focused on the problem alone:

"The open door is letting in the cold."

"The dog needs to be let out."

"The mess needs to be cleaned up now."

By simply describing the facts—what has happened or what needs to be done—your child's attention stays on her mistake rather than on your reaction to it.

"Why isn't the table set yet? How many times have I told you . . ." directs your child's attention to your anger. "The table needs to be set before we can eat," directs her attention to what needs to be done.

"The rug needs to be cleaned. The vacuum is in the closet."

Describe the problem or what needs to done, then step away. Keep your child focused on the problem.

In the unlikely case that your child really doesn't understand how irritated or angry you are, you can describe your anger or frustration at a later time when he is more likely to be open to hearing what you have to say.

"It is very frustrating to have to remind you to close the door each morning. What do you think would help you remember tomorrow?"

This conversation can take place later. But in the moment, describing the problem alone will be more effective in correcting the misbehavior and moving on.

Describe the problem without using "you"

By avoiding the word "you," the focus remains on the problem and the solution rather than the people involved.

If your five year-old jumps on the clean laundry and spills it all over the floor, respond with:

"The clothes need to be picked up and put in the basket."

If wet swimsuits are left on the couch, respond with:

"Wet swimsuits go in the laundry."

When bikes are left outside again, say "Bikes need to be put in the garage."

Describe the problem and the solution

Recall one thing your child does that you often respond to with extended criticism or ridicule:

_____

_____

Now simply describe what the problem is or what needs to take place, without criticism or condescension. Avoid using the word "you:"

_____

_____

If said firmly, stating the problem alone will accomplish at least as much as an angry tirade and probably more.

Demonstrate when words don't work

If it seems like you could tell your child a thousand times to not hit when she gets angry and still she would never learn it, you may be right. Some children learn by being told. Many children, however, learn only by what they see. They will never get it by words alone.

If you want to teach your daughter to step back when she is angry, clap her hands together forcefully, and say, "That really makes me mad," demonstrate. She may be a child who learns better from what she sees than from what she hears described in words.

Picture a new way

Other children who don't learn by words alone can be shown new behaviors by teaching them visualization.

"Imagine yourself beginning to get angry. Now see yourself stepping back, taking a deep breath, and saying 'I'm upset right now; we'll talk about this later.'"

Being told a better way to behave is only a half-step for many children. Modeling and visualizing help them picture themselves responding in a new way and will greatly increase the chance they will try new behaviors.

Consider either technique—demonstrating what you say or having the child visualize it—to begin to show your child a different way to behave. If you've already said something "a hundred times" but haven't seen any difference, it's time to try something new.

Children learn from other children

Another way to teach new skills to children who must see to learn is by connecting them with another child who has already mastered the skill.

Every skill your child needs to learn, some other child knows. The trick is to create an opportunity for your child to see the other child in action. If the task is something simple like cleaning a room, it may be easy to arrange for your "organizationally challenged" child to be with another child when cleaning is the chore of the moment.

More complicated social skills, such as sharing materials or following the rules of a game, can also be learned by asking another child to help. Never underestimate children's willingness to help each other if they understand exactly what needs to be taught.

"John seems to have trouble understanding the rules for this game. Could you explain to him what you know so he doesn't get in fights as often?"

Many children will learn from other kids more easily than from you or any other adult. Other children may, in fact, understand what your child needs to learn even better than you do. It's worth a try.

You could simply put them together at the right time and hope that learning takes place. Or could you ask the child directly to teach your child or at least to give some help. Not all children are capable of this, but many will enjoy being put in the position of teacher and will welcome the chance to help.

Demonstrate when words don't work

What is something that your child has trouble learning or doing?

_____

_____

How could you demonstrate the behavior you would like to see?

_____

_____

How could you help your child visualize the new behavior?

_____

_____

Name another child who has no difficulty doing this and who might be willing to help:

_____

Tell a story that makes your point

When misbehavior seems to result from a lack of understanding—how it feels to be teased, the consequences of cheating, how to handle a bully —telling a story of how you learned this lesson can be your most valuable teaching tool:

"When I was your age, I was bothered by a bully . . ."

Lessons from your life create a much more powerful lesson than simply telling the child what you think he should know or feel or do. Children enjoy hearing that you faced similar problems as a child. It is often best to just tell the story, without explaining what should be learned from it. Just tell the story:

"I had trouble with a bully in kindergarten. What I did was . . ."

Stories of other people's lives can be powerful as well:

"There was a boy I knew in third grade who . . ."

Stories are more effective and lasting than lectures because they create images in children's minds of actual people facing the struggles they are up against. Stories don't need to tell children what to do but only to suggest a possible solution and let them know that others have faced this problem and survived.

Proverbs, fables, and allegories are also valuable in guiding children toward more positive behavior. Though taught less often in schools today, the truths they contain remain as valid and insightful as ever:

"Do you recall the story of the coyote and the bear?"

Responding to misbehavior with stories and anecdotes is particularly useful for children who don't like to be confronted with what they have done wrong or who resist being told directly what they should do.

In the past decade, a multitude of books have been written to help children deal with specific problems of childhood. Your school or public librarian can suggest books on topics ranging from standing up to bullies to dealing with the death of a loved one. In your local library, you will also find books of fables, including modern fables from all segments of our society and from around the world.

The school counselor is another good source for books and materials on counseling or therapy issues. Ensure that the reading level and content are geared to the age of your child.

Books provide an useful avenue to subjects that you may not feel comfortable discussing with your child.

Teach with a story
What is one lesson or one virtue you would like to teach to your child?

_____

_____

What story from your childhood might help teach it?

_____

_____

Give the school library a call, and ask if they have any books that deal specifically with that topic:

_____

_____

If you have time, look in a quote book for thoughts you could use to make your point using other peoples words or anecdotes.

In many cultures, positive behavior is taught primarily through stories and anecdotes. Your child may find that reading about what other children in the world value will provide unique insights into an old problem.

Make or take a time-out that works

Time-out—excluding a child from your attention—is a useful response to some misbehavior, but it should not be a universal response to all misbehavior.

The assumption behind using time-outs is that removing your child to a location away from your attention will cause him to reconsider his actions and want to come back. In some cases this works well; the child does want to come back and will not misbehave upon his return.

Other times, however, he enjoys being away, particularly if doesn't like the kids he was playing with or doesn't enjoy what he was doing. In these situations, a time-out won't be effective because it's exactly what he wants.

Sending a child away from you for a minute or two of time-out is most valuable in two circumstances: 1) when the child clearly enjoys what he is doing and will be eager to return, and 2) to interrupt escalating anger. When your child misbehaves, send her to sit by the wall or anywhere convenient, continue with what you are doing, and after a short time—one to four minutes—invite her to return with a reminder of the behavior you expect.

Time-out is a useful intervention, but beware of overusing it. If imposing a time-out creates more problems than it solves, try another approach.

Offer yourself a time-out

When anger escalates, giving yourself a time-out, stepping to another room for a few minutes, may work just as well as sending your child away.

A time-out can be brief

Originally it was said that children should be sent to a special location for a set number of minutes—generally one minute for each year of age. If this works for you and your child, that's great, but if getting a child to go to a special time-out location for a set number of minutes only escalates the misconduct, it may not be worth the trouble. Consider the following variations:

Time-out can be as simple as having your child stop where he is and freeze for a moment or sit down on the floor. Thirty seconds or a minute may be all that is needed to interrupt misbehavior at any age. The time-out should end as soon as a change in energy or attitude is evident and before boredom or anger kick in.

Time-out for a highly active child can be created by simply kneeling in front of the child and firmly holding her arms until she slows down enough to return to what she was doing—probably less than a minute—or by turning her chair away from the table for as little as twenty to forty seconds. Younger children can be held on your lap—again, only for as long as it takes to interrupt the activity or calm the energy.

You can create a time-out in many ways that do not depend on your child's willingness to participate. Time-out can be thirty seconds while you stand in front of the TV. Time-out can be one minute with the lights off. Or if your child is rambunctious at bedtime, it can be thirty seconds while you stand silently in the room with the light on. Time-out can be pulling your car to the side of the road; nothing needs to be said.

Time-out creates a pause in the action, but you cannot assume that it teaches your child a new way to behave—a better way to handle his anger, or how to play fairly in a group. Time-out does not teach new skills, and that is its greatest limitation. After a time-out, ask yourself what your child needs to learn to stay out of trouble the next time.

Create a time-out that works for your child

When does your child's behavior seem to escalate most? On what occasion would you most want to interrupt the action and create a new beginning?

_____

_____

What kind of time-out would be effective for your child? Is your child compliant enough, even when angry, to go away to a chair or a wall?

_____

_____

Would going to the bedroom be effective, or is it simply an entertaining reward?

_____

_____

Would holding her be enough? Or standing beside him?

_____

Defuse with a positive assumption

When your daughter walks across the carpet with muddy boots or returns home later than the agreed-upon time, you can respond from one of two assumptions.

You can assume that she knew what she did was wrong and that she did it just to test you. In that case, you'll probably jump down her throat:

"How many times have I told you to take off your boots? Are you trying to make me mad again? Well, it's working!"

"You know you're late. Don't you know how to tell time?"

Such accusatory statements, "You're doing this on purpose!" and insulting questions, "Can't you tell time?" can do more harm to your relationship than the misbehavior itself.

Or you can respond from a more positive assumption—that she didn't know or simply forgot—and direct your comments only to what now needs to take place.

"Your feet are muddy. Walk back outside and take off your boots. The rag to clean up the floor is under the sink."

"It's after eight o'clock. You may have forgotten the time, but as we agreed, there will be no TV and you will go directly to your room."

The response you choose will tell your child a lot about your feelings and assumptions.

By assuming innocence, you show that you are willing to believe she may have forgotten but still expect her to take responsibility for her mistake.

Of course, your positive assumption may be wrong; she may know exactly what she did, and she may have done it to make you angry. Acting from positive assumptions is not about being right; it is about providing an opportunity for your child to correct her mistake with a reminder rather than an accusation. If the misbehavior continues, you will have other opportunities to come down hard.

If a positive assumption results in your child taking responsibility, then it was as effective as any reprimand could have been.

"You forgot you needed to complete your homework first, but there is probably time for you to do it before the show begins."

You may not always be correct, but you will avoid the lasting damage that a false accusation can create.

Assume innocence or forgetfulness

The following sentences provide examples of assuming innocence or forgetfulness:

If the table wasn't set for dinner, "Remember it's your night to set the table."

If the VCR was left on all night, "The video needs to be turned off at night."

If your child tracks mud through the house, "Your shoes were muddier than you thought; the mop is in the closet."

If you find a wall covered with crayon drawings, "These walls can't be written on. They need to be scrubbed now."

Positive assumptions allow you to say what needs to be done without making an assumption about whether the misdeed was done intentionally or accidentally. Assume the best, direct what needs to be done, and move on.

Practice positive assumptions

Think of something your child has done recently that made you angry:

_____

_____

Now, imagine that your child was completely innocent. Imagine—
and this might take a lot of imagination—that your child honestly
had no idea this was wrong or completely forgot that you had told
him about this at least a hundred times. If that's difficult, imagine the
misdeed was done by another child, a child from a foreign country or
planet. What would you say to make your point without assuming
intentional wrongdoing?

_____

_____

By making no assumptions about your child's intentions, there is no
need for anger. Simply state what was done wrong or what needs to
be done and move on:

"By the way, we store the hammer in the tool box not up there on
the roof."

Remember, this is not about being right in your assumption, it is
about making your point and moving on.

Share power through choice

If you tire of constantly telling children what to do, it's time to get good at offering choices. Choices allow children to make their own decisions within the acceptable limits you offer. Children feel competent as they select from two options that are both agreeable to you.

"Do you want to play five minutes on the swing or on the slide?"

"Will you brush your teeth before or after a story tonight?"

Which option they choose doesn't really matter to you. Either way you get what you need: five minutes of play and teeth brushed. The secret to wisely using options is to make sure that both options are acceptable to you and reasonable to your child:

"Do want your broccoli cooked or raw tonight?" It's broccoli either way.

"Do you want to do your homework before or after dinner tonight?" Either way the homework is to be done.

Offering choices shows your children that you respect their opinions and judgments and helps avoid arguments over simple matters.

Choices can be used to prevent problems before they occur:

"Do you want to play in the front yard or the back yard today?"

Playing in the street—what the child probably had in mind—was not presented as an option.

Threats are not choices

Try to avoid offering choices that are really only veiled threats. If the second choice is clearly unpleasant, this is not a choice—merely a threat.

"You can finish your homework or be grounded for two weeks."

This is not a choice, it is an order with the threat of punishment attached to it.

The following examples offer two sets of options.

You want your child to wash his face:

"Do you want to wash your face or do you want me to?"

"Do you want to wash your face now or after we finish the story?"

You want your ten-year-old daughter to wear a dress for a family wedding:

"Do you want to wear your red dress or the new blue one?"

"Do you want to change into your dress now or when we get to Grandma's house?"

You want your five-year-old to eat green beans:

"Do you want to eat the beans right away or after you try the meat?"

"Do you want ten beans or fifteen?"

Plan for choices in your home

Think of something you must repeatedly remind your child to do:

_____

_____

Now, what choices, acceptable to you, could you offer your child. Remember, the idea is to give your child some say in what she must do.

What are two choices you could give regarding when she does it?

Do you want to do it _____

or would you prefer to do it _____

Now give two choices regarding what she does.

Do you want to choose _____

or would you rather choose _____

Imagine a positive intention

Suppose your child left food all over the living room floor. You could be severe in your response, accusing the child of trying to make you angry, or you could surprise the child by giving the problem a positive intention.

"Thanks for the reminder that it's time for us to clean the house this evening."

Reframing the situation helps you set aside your emotional reaction to your child's behavior, especially if it has become antagonistic. Imagining a positive intention behind even the most negative behavior can turn the head of even a belligerent child. Humor is important.

"You're right, my hair does look awful today, and I appreciate you reminding me to make an appointment for a cut. Thanks."

"I guess it is a messy desk. Help me put some of this junk on the back table."

Make the best of what has occurred by using the problem as a reminder or an opportunity to work together.

"This is a good opportunity for us spend some time together cleaning up."

Reframing makes a young child's intentional misbehavior seem helpful and can reduce your own tendency to feel hurt by what your child says.

"I'm sure you call me 'fat' to remind me to get exercise, right? Thanks, let's take a walk together after lunch. Exercise will be good for both of us."

Maintaining your cool—doing the unusual when your child expects you to blow up—is an effective response to deliberately offensive behavior.

Here are some additional examples of reframing.

Your teenager leaves the door unlocked all night. You could say:

"Now we know the burglars aren't checking our door every night,"

or "This is a good chance for us to talk about other safety concerns in the neighborhood."

You get a call from your child's teacher about homework not being done, you could say:

"This is a great chance for us to talk about how your other classes are going as well."

Try unpredictable responses

Think of a recent comment that seemed to be deliberately offensive:

_____

_____

What could you have "imagined" as a positive intention for your child's behavior? What could you have said to your child?

Thanks for the_____

_____

or, I bet you said that to _____

_____

How could you have described it as an opportunity?

Thanks for saying that. This is a great opportunity for us to _____

_____

Punishment is not an effective way to change behavior

Punishment does make a person regret getting caught, but too often it leaves in its wake an angry child looking for an opportunity to get back at you.

When punishment has no logical connection to the offense—for example, when a spanking is the punishment for throwing a ball at a baby—children come to feel that the punishment cancels out any need to feel guilty—in this case, for endangering the baby. The child focuses his thoughts on the punishment rather than on the wrong he did in the first place.

Appropriate consequences, such as taking the ball away, show the child that an act of misbehavior will result in some corrective action to reduce the likelihood that the misbehavior will reoccur:

"Because it has been damaged again, the bike will be put away until next week."

Consequences may either have a set time to them (no bike until next week) or be contingent upon some kind of reparation:

"The skates were left outside last night. They will stay inside the house until they are cleaned up."

Arguments the child might raise provide you with an opportunity to restate why the consequence was imposed in the first place:

"The bike has been put away for two days because it was misused."

Or you can explain what will remove the consequence:

"The skates can go outside again after they are cleaned."

Effective consequences are understandable

To be effective, consequences must come directly from yur child's action in a way that he can understand and hopefully will learn from. Consequences focus his thoughts on what he did and what he needs to do to correct it.

While your child may still be angry with you, most children will recognize that your response was designed to teach them something, not just to inflict pain upon them for making a mistake.

Misbehavior—an opportunity

Punishment seldom meets the need that may have prompted the misbehavior in the first place—the need for more positive attention, alternative activities, or time together with you.

Incidents of misbehavior provide you with an opportunity to require your child to do something. She probably expects to have to do something unpleasant to make up for what she did wrong. But you have a marvelous opportunity to requireher to do something that you know would be good for her. In other words, you can design a consequence that meets your child's inner needs.

Next time your child is caught doing something wrong, ask yourself what you can require her to do that would actually be good for her.

If she broke your screwdriver trying to take apart an old radio, you could require her to fix something else that she might really enjoy learning about?

If she damaged a table while running around the house, the punishment could be five minutes on your exercise bike or a five-minute jog around the inner courtyard of your apartment building. Those activities would meet the need to burn off energy.

If you believe your child is making noise so you will stop work and pay attention to her, the need-meeting consequence could be a request to help you clean up your office.

When your child expects to be punished, you have a perfect

opportunity to require her to do something she might enjoy more than misbehavior.

Consider alternatives to punishment in your home

Consider a recent incident of misbehavior that you responded to with a punishment of some sort.

The incident: _____

_____

The punishment: _____

_____

Now create a consequence that would require your child to do something she normally wouldn't do but might actually enjoy:

_____

_____

Select an activity that would meet the need that may have prompted the misbehavior —a physical activity, time with you, sharing a fun activity with a sibling, anything that might build skills and connections with others rather than just punish.

_____

_____

A need-meeting consequence is anything that would ultimately be good for your child—meet a need inside—even though she might not see it that way at the moment.

Focus on a solution

If the car is scratched as a bike is taken out of the garage, your first
thought may be how to punish the child who caused the damage. This,
however, is an ideal moment to make a plan that will keep this from
happening again. After all, isn't that what is most important, not having the problem reoccur?

Focusing immediately on a solution gives you a moment to calm
your anger and confront the problem. Inviting the child to be involved
in brainstorming a solution will give you further time to think about
how you want to respond.

"Can you think of a way . . . ?" is a good question to ask.

Children often have the perfect solution and are more likely to
follow through on a solution that they suggest.

Or if you have a suggestion, offer it right away, while your child
is still concerned and wondering how much trouble he has gotten
into. By focusing on a solution first, you avoid falling into the "detail trap," in which all of your energy is spent talking about the details of the past incident rather than what will prevent it from happening again.

With a plan in place to avoid a reoccurrence, you and your child
will be calmer and better able to think together about how to repair the
damage that has been done. You can avoid thinking that some pain-
producing punishment is needed to keep the incident from happening
again.

"Sounds like you now know how to get your bike out the side door. After you go with me to the body shop to see what repairs will cost, we'll talk about how you can help pay for the damage."

Teaching your child how to correct problems and how to forgive mistakes will be more valuable than demonstrating how to inflict pain upon those who displease you.

In the following examples, let your thoughts go immediately to what is needed to fix the problem rather than what would punish the offense:

If the couch is torn because children jumped on it, you might suggest: "As a special treat, we can place mattresses on the bedroom floor. Now about this couch . . . "

If books are lost on the way home from school, you might suggest: "Let's think of somewhere safe to place your books while you are playing."

If a picture is broken when a basketball is thrown in the house, try offering: "Tomorrow we'll go to the park and we can shoot baskets together. In the meantime you can fix that frame."

Plan to discuss solutions in your home

Consider a recent behavior that you punished in some manner:

_____

_____

After the punishment, did you spend time with your child, discussing how to avoid the problem next time?

_____

_____

If not, what could you have suggested to avoid it happening again?

_____

_____

Might you have come up with a different punishment if you had first come up with a solution?

_____

_____

Next time, resolve to first discuss a solution that will work in the future before you begin discussing what to do about the past.

Ask the second question

Does this sound familiar? You're checking the fit of a new pair of pants in the department store mirror. The salesperson says, "Those pants are just right for you. Will that be cash or credit?" The salesperson is using a simple sales technique called "asking the second question" to move you to purchase. The first and most obvious question, "Do you want to buy the pants?" isn't even asked. The salesperson jumps over that question and directs your attention to the second question: will that be cash or credit? If he can get you to answer this second question, he has a sale.

In the same way you can learn to "ask the second question" to direct your child to what needs to be done.

The living room is a mess and you have company coming. Skip over the first question, "Are you going to clean up your mess?" and ask the second question:

"After you clean the living room, do you want to help me make dessert or set the table?" or

"When you are done picking up the living room, do you want to go back outside until your cousins arrive?"

You assume rather than ask for compliance by directing the child's thoughts to what comes next. Here's another example:

"After you have finished your homework, which story would you like to read?"

Asking the second question (instead of the first) helps reduce noncompliance by walking your child toward an acceptable option. It works as well at home as it does in the store.

A couple more examples may help you find the right words to begin asking the second question.

If you need your daughter to change an offensive t-shirt before you
take her to school, ask:

"After you change into an acceptable shirt, shall we . . . "

When it's time for your son to take his allergy medicine, ask:

"After you take your medicine, do you want to . . . "

With time, you can be just as good at this process as salespeople are.

Develop second questions

Think of something you will probably want your child to do this evening:

_____

_____

Rather than asking her to do it or asking if she will do it, think of a
second question you can ask:

_____

_____

The secret is to assume she will do what is needed, and move her attention right on to what follows.

For more practice, think of a task you might want your child to do later
this week:

_____

Now ask the second question:

_____

_____

Do the unexpected

Often the most effective response to misbehavior is the most unexpected response. If the misbehavior has been a routine problem, then you have undoubtedly fallen into a routine response as well. If your child always complains about having to ride in the back seat, chances are you always offer the same response:

"Just do what I say."

"Stop whining. All kids ride in back."

Now, what would be the most unexpected response you could give?

You could say, "Yes. Of course you can ride in the front. Today is Tuesday the 14th; every Tuesday the 14th you can ride in front at least once."

Or you could respond with humor when you usually would respond with anger.

"Of course you don't like what we are having for dinner. This was your sister's day to pick the meal. This is your day to not like what we eat."

Or you could write a note rather than repeat the same old lecture. A note on the bed, "Remember how good it feels to crawl into a made bed at night?" is less likely to begin an argument.

The most unexpected response may be to change your expectation, to give less attention to one concern and more attention to another. Step back and see if a situation might change if it received less rather than more attention.

Try an unexpected response

Think of one recurring problem and your usual response:

_____

_____

If you were to just try something different next time, what would be the opposite of your usual response? What would be the most unexpected response you could make?

_____

_____

Does this problem deserve the time and energy you are giving it or should you let it go for now?

_____

_____

Avoid "never," "always," and names

In any argument, there are certain words that serve only to insult—words that escalate tension. Avoiding the use of those escalating words and teaching your child not to use them won't eliminate conflict, but it will keep arguments directed toward solutions rather than heading toward explosions.

The words "never" and "always" are escalating words. Saying "you never" or "you always" or "every day you " escalates difficulties because these phrases usually exaggerate the problem and are seldom accurate. Does your child always, every single time, lose things when he borrows them? If not, he will recall the one time he did return an item and will immediately become defensive, insisting, "I don't always lose stuff," and the point of your discussion will be lost.

Teach children by your example to state exactly what was done and when. Then the argument can avoid exaggeration and stay on track.

"Last Thursday you took the shirt I laid out on my bed to wear."

"Last Saturday you came in forty-five minutes after I asked you to."

Name-calling, another escalator

Name-calling is lazy criticism: instead of taking the time to describe exactly what angered you, you label the person with an offensive name. As soon as name-calling begins, "You're a brat," the conversation switches from discussing the problem and potential solutions to defense and counterattack: "I am not a brat, you're the brat."

Again, direct your children from name-calling to a description of the problem or what they are feeling:

"You call her a pain, because she did what?"

"Tell me what you are upset about."

Teach your children to describe what happened and how they feel without exaggeration or name-calling. This will avoid escalating anger.

Avoid absolutes

If you or your children are in the habit of using "always" or "never," you might need some practice changing these absolutes to more specific language.

If your child's room is a mess, you might typically say, "Your room is always a mess. You never clean up after yourself."

Try a simple change, "Your room is often a mess. You rarely clean up after yourself."

Better yet, describe what you see, "Your room is messy today."

Best of all, describe what needs to be done, "Your clothes need to be hung up, your toys put away, and your bed made."

Avoid labels

Even words parents use to label common behaviors, words like "whining, or lying," will be more effective if they are more specific.

Rather than saying, "Stop whining," try saying, "Talk to me in a voice that I will listen to—in a big boy voice."

Rather than saying, "Stop lying," try saying, "Tell me what actually happened, not what you wish had happened."

Being specific yourself and teaching your child to be specific in describing problems will avoid the most common of all anger escalators: over-emotionalizing the problem.

Reduce a name-calling habit

The best way to eliminate name-calling is to insist on better descriptions. To change a long-standing name-calling habit, you can, at first, allow the word but use it with "is being" rather than "is." Instead of

"You are a pain," switch to "You are being a pain." This is a step in a better direction because it begins to focus the name-calling on the moment not the person, saying in essence:

"You aren't always a pain, but you are being a pain at this moment."

As a next step, insist that any name be attached to a specific behavior:

"He is a brat when he takes my clothes without telling me."

After some practice with the first two steps, you can move toward allowing no name-calling at all, teaching your children to describe what they are feeling, not what they think the other person is being:

"I get very upset when I set out clothes to wear and then you take them."

Teaching your child to avoid name-calling will make arguments much easier to resolve for the rest of their lives.

Eliminate name-calling in your home

Think of an insulting name that you sometimes use with your child:

_____

Now use it in a sentence beginning with, You are being:

_____

Now use the same name, but make it even more specific by beginning the sentence with:

You are a _____ when you _____

The final goal is to say what you feel:

I don't like it when you _____

Now repeat this process as you think of your child's name-calling.

Think of an insulting name that your child sometimes uses:

_____

Now use it in a sentence beginning with, You are being:

_____

Now use the same name, but make it even more specific by beginning the sentence with:

You are a _____ when you _____

The final goal is for your child to be able to say what she feels:

I don't like it when you _____

Helping your children to be more specific in their name-calling is a step toward eliminating name-calling all together. The sooner name-calling is completely eliminated, the sooner children will learn to resolve rather than escalate difficulties.

Defusing Anger

It's difficult to deal with an angry child. If you can deflect conflict before it arises or defuse anger before an explosion, you can effectively reduce the difficulties you would otherwise encounter.

Say "yes" and "when"

No one likes to hear the word "no." Some kids let their emotions escalate immediately upon hearing "no" and stop listening to any further explanations. If you notice that your child gets angry the instant the word "no" comes out of your mouth, try saying it a different way. In response to, "Can I go to the movie tonight?" (a school night), try "Yes, you can go to the movie . . . on the weekend." "Yes, you can go outside, after you finish your homework." Saying "yes" and then stating the rule or conditions avoids the harshness of the word "no." More important, it provides you with an opportunity to remind the person of the specifics of the rule. It also draws the child's mind off the "no" of the moment and toward to the circumstances of a future "yes." Even "yes, you can have a new bike . . . next year," gives something to look forward to.

"But" is also a stopper

Another word that can stop your child from hearing the words that follow is "but." "Yes, you are dressed warmly, but you can't go outside this late at night." To which the child answers "But, why?" Somehow explaining with the word "but" just invites argument. So avoid using it. Use "and" instead of "but" when confronting arguments against a rule you are not willing to negotiate. "Yes, I know you would go to bed right after the movie . . . and . . . movies are only allowed on weekends." "You do watch well for cars . . . and . . . two-year-olds walk across the street with their mothers.

The word "and" shows that what the child believes he will do and what you feel needs to be done can exist together. "I don't disagree with what you say . . . and . . . this is the way it has to be." Using the word "and" rather than the word "but" states the disagreement without inviting further discussion. When you avoid using the words "no" and "but," you will avoid many angry challenges from your child.

The following examples show how you can deny permission for requests using "yes," and stating the rule rather than "no."

"May I walk downtown tonight?"

"Yes, you can walk downtown . . . first thing in the morning."

"Can I have a second piece of pie."

"Sure you can . . . tomorrow at supper time."

Prepare to say "yes" and "when" in your home

Practice saying "yes" and "when" instead of "but" in the following sentences:

Your four-year-old asks for a pocket knife.

You say, "You can't have a knife at age four."

Your child says, "Dad, I promise to be careful."

You say, "Yes, I know you would, and _____

_____

Try it with a typical example from your home.

Your child asks _____

You say, "Yes, _____

and _____

Defuse with a choice

When your child angrily refuses to do what you ask, you can threaten with punishment, "If you don't . . . I'll . . . ," but offering a choice will probably go a lot farther toward getting you what you want at the moment. In the face of confrontation, offering a choice is often the fastest way to resolution.

"I will not clean up the bedroom, and you can't make me."

"You can clean up the bedroom as I've asked, or you can help me with the dishes. You choose."

Offering choices defuses power struggles by giving the child a say in what he does while still getting you, more or less, what you need. Guiding a child's choices between two acceptable options is the first step in teaching wise decision making.

"Do you want to hold my hand or grab my coat as we across the road ?"

"You can walk to the car, or I will carry you."

Avoid demands by offering options

While offering choices is helpful after a conflict has occurred, it is best used before a conflict arises to direct your child's thoughts to acceptable options.

To avoid demands for a chocolate candy bar, as you enter the store, you might say:

"You may have a piece of gum or a licorice today. Which do you want?"

If your child often insists on taking a noisy electronic toy to a restaurant, before you get ready to leave, ask:

"Do you want to leave the roboto in your room or on the table so you'll remember it as soon as we get back?"

To reduce nightly arguments about bedtime routines, try:

"Do you want to brush your teeth before or after I do this evening?"

Offering choices defuses power struggles by giving strong-willed children more than just "comply or be punished." Complying without question is not what a determined child is inclined to do. Teaching children to make wise choices will serve you both much better.

A few more examples will prepare you to offer choices in your home.

You need your child to wash his face for school:

"Do you want to wash your face before or after you get dressed?"

The floor needs to be swept:

"Do you want to sweep the floor before or after dinner?"

He's headed for the toy department, you're willing to buy candy, not a toy:

"Do you want a candy bar or an ice cream cone today?"

He wants an ice cream cone, you only have money for gum: "Do you want one piece of gum or two today?"

Prepare to offer choices in your home

Consider a recent time that you struggled to get your child to do what you needed him to do, preferably a situation that you may face again tomorrow:

_____

_____

Could have offered your child two different times to have done what was necessary? Could you next time offer:

Do you want to do this _____or _____

Could you have offered two different options?

Do you want to _____ or _____

Now think of a situation coming up when you know your child will want to do something you can't allow her to do, for whatever reason:

_____

_____

Before the situation arises, offer two choices to distract her from the unacceptable option she probably will have in mind:

You can either _____ or _____

Calm your body and just listen

By becoming aware of how anger builds in your body, both you and your child can learn to stay in control when conflict arises.

What is your body's first sign of rising anger? If you first feel your fists begin to clench, take this as a signal to step back, shake off the tension in your hands, and take a deep breath before speaking.

If your voice rises when irritated, at this first signal determine to hold your voice low, even switching to a whisper if that is helpful. A determined whisper can be at least as forceful and attention-getting as shouting. Practicing a determined quiet voice will also help you avoid the urge to outshout your child, which would only increase the tension in both of you. Avoid confronting gestures—clenching a fist, pounding on a table, or standing over your child in way that evokes fear. Once afraid, a child's thinking begins to shut down. Make it a habit to sit down when angry or kneel down to the child's level.

You can also control the timing of your comments. If you fear losing control, just listen. Let your child have his say while you regain your composure. Try to find something in what he is saying that you can agree with.

You may even want to step outside before you say anything at all. Do something incompatible with anger; take a walk and return when your body has calmed down.

Above all, if you know immediately that you may not be able to control your reaction, think one thought only: Get out! Walk away before you do or say anything at all. Do whatever is necessary to calm your body before you do harm.

Deep breathing is a quick relaxation technique

When anxious or excited, we tend to take short, shallow breaths high in the chest. This type of breathing stimulates rather than relaxes the body. Therefore, to relax, take a slow breath deep into your abdomen. Then exhale slowly. Continue with a few more deep breaths to further calm your body.

Each time you inhale, tighten the muscles in your hands, then slowly release as you exhale. Tighten then release the tension in all the other areas of your body that you have learned to associate with rising tension: your shoulders, forehead, and particularly your jaw.

Practice control

Think about one situation in the near future in which it may be difficult for you to control your anger:

_____

What might be your first signal that your anger is rising?

_____

What is one thing you might do to help yourself stay in control?

_____

_____

If that doesn't work, what will be your second signal that you are near the edge of losing control?

_____

_____

What step might you take at that time, something that may not resolve the situation but will give you time to get back in control?

_____

Stay directive not destructive

In a moment of anger, it is easy to become destructive: to say and do things that may damage your relationship with your child more than the child's misbehavior. Often these responses are automatic, impulsive reactions that you learned as a child.

To keep an argument from becoming destructive, stay instructive in what you say. Instruct your child in what you feel or what you want without sarcasm or expressions of disgust that will hurt her long after the argument is over.

Rather than, "Do you think you can listen now?" heavily laden with sarcasm, simply instruct what you need:

"I need you to listen now."

Instruct in the consequences of misbehavior without destructive, frightening threats, which reduce your credibility:

"Not being home on time will result in having to stay in tomorrow night."

Finally, be firm in your instruction. Give power to what you say by not discussing it endlessly. Have a plan in place if what you expect isn't done and stick with the plan.

Rather than destructive sarcasm, groans of disgust, or idle threats, simply stay instructive: say what needs to happen and the consequences if it doesn't happen. Say it once. As you respond to anger in this way, your child will learn that conflict does not need to be destructive.

Don't pile on

To remain instructive rather than destructive, avoid piling on multiple reprimands when your child has done something wrong. If your child is feeling bad about what she has done, this is not the time to launch into a string of ten things you are upset about.

"And you never . . . "

"And last week, you . . . "

Doing this will only remove your child's attention from the current offense and cause her to ignore everything you are saying. Stay with one concern. And when you have both had your say or resolved that issue, let it go and move on.

Practice being directive in your home

Think back to a recent incident in which you became angry. Recall all that you said, and how the argument played out:

_____

_____

_____

_____

Looking back, how could you have said in one sentence what needed to happen or what you needed your child to do?

_____

_____

If you think a consequence needed to be stated, what could you have said would be the result if the child didn't do what was needed?

_____

_____

Finally, instead of becoming destructive in language, imagine yourself simply restating what needs to happen. Practice saying it just once.

Reveal the emotion behind the anger

To control anger in your family, teach yourself and your children to express feelings with words rather than actions.

"I am very angry that you broke this tool."

"I am furious about this mess, and I expect it to be cleaned up immediately."

State your feeling briefly and authoritatively rather than making a verbal attack on your child. One sentence can be enough to defuse anger that might otherwise be expressed physically.

"Seeing this makes me very frustrated."

"I'm angry that I have to tell you again."

Look for the feelings

As you express your feelings with words, try to recognize the hidden emotions behind your anger. Fear, anxiety, and worry often underlie anger when a child is not home on time. An angry outburst probably reflects your fear of what could have happened. Describing your worry rather than your anger will give your child a better understanding of why her being on time is important to you.

"I was worried to death that you could have been hurt. You know the problems in that neighborhood at night."

Anger can reflect your feeling of helplessness at not being able to control your child's every behavior and your expectation that you should be able to. Getting in touch with the underlying emotion can help you moderate your anger toward your child.

"When I call you in a store and you walk away, I don't feel I can keep you safe. I can't have that when we're in the mall."

Feelings of inadequacy can be the source of unreasonable anger when your child gets hurt. Are you angry at what your child did or at your inability to prevent him from hurting himself?

Acknowledging the hidden emotion behind your reaction can help you better control how you respond to the child:

"I feel worried/frustrated/resentful/disappointed/afraid . . . "

When you express the feelings that underlie your anger, you will help your child recognize and be able to express the fears behind his anger.

Say so if you're sorry

Overreaction to a child's misbehavior can come from any number of feelings. You may see a child's mistake as a reflection of an emotion you still struggle with. If so, you may overreact because you're angry at yourself. Regardless of what the feeling is behind an overreaction, here are some things you can say to acknowledge that you lost it and hope to do better next time. Repeat each aloud, just for practice:

"Sorry I blew up at you."

"I wish I hadn't said . . . "

"I feel less angry now and wish I hadn't . . . "

A simple apology can help you both move beyond the angry destructive words that were said, and it will remind you to be more careful next time.

Identify your emotions

On the following page, make a list of the times you have gotten angry in the last days, weeks, or months.

Next to each item, record what might have been the hidden emotion behind the anger. Here are a few reminders: You may have been worried, frustrated, resentful, disappointed, afraid, helpless, discouraged, or overwhelmed.

Incident	Emotion
_____	_____
_____	_____
_____	_____
_____	_____
_____	_____
_____	_____
_____	_____
_____	_____
_____	_____

Taking time to identify the emotions underlying your anger helps you better describe those emotions to your child. Teaching these words helps your child to better express his anger to you.

Speak, then move with action

Your words are only as persuasive as the child's belief that, if necessary, your words will be followed with action. This is easiest to establish when your child is young. A preschool child who has been told to go outside once, or maybe twice, and who still refuses can be shown the way with action.

Hold your child firmly by the shoulders and walk him out. If he resists more than you can physically manage or feel comfortable with, stop. Assign a time-out and wait for him to regain control.

As your child grows older, it will be more effective to present physical action as a choice you are considering:

"You can walk to the door, or I can take you there. You choose."

This is not really a choice, it's more like a threat. But as a final chance to avoid having to take action, it can be very effective. If you offer this choice, you will find out how important it is to your child to resist your direction. Then you can either follow through physically, or you can recognize that your child is very determined to resist. If so, you may want to step back and reconsider the importance you give to compliance at the moment:

"I would prefer to not have to drag you out of this store. Tell me again, what is so important about going back to the toy area."

Above all, avoid threats that you have no intention of following through on:

"If you don't move, I'll throw you through that door head first."

Using physical action is a last resort, but when children are young, it's indispensable to establish your willingness to follow through and compel them to follow your instructions.

After a certain age, however, physical follow-through is no longer possible or effective. When to stop depends on the age and physical strength of your child and the degree of resistance you feel you can safely manage. If taking action can't be done safely, it shouldn't be done at all. With older children your follow-through must be with the power of persuasion or with consequences you can still enforce.

Physical restraint

If your child regularly loses control, violently attacking you or others or endangering himself, you may need to learn how to physically restrain him.

Physical restraint is a professional, therapeutic procedure that involves holding an out-of-control child immobile in a specific manner. It is not a disciplinary response. It is done exclusively to protect the child's safety. For this reason, it is beyond the scope of this book to provide instruction for its use. Instruction may be available through local mental health services or psychiatric facilities. Training should involve numerous hours of professional instruction by an experienced or licensed practitioner.

Prepare to follow through

Practice saying the following sentences, in an attempt to avoid having to step in with physical action:

"You can walk to the car, or I will place you in the car."

"Can you leave the store on your own, or do I need to help you?"

"You can walk in, or I can carry you in. Which do you choose?"

In what situation might you need to take physical action?

_____

_____

What could you say to make it clear that you will follow through?

_____

_____

What action will you take if your child does not comply?

_____

_____

Suggest a way out

Before you dive in with a long lecture, consider the possibility that the lesson has already been learned.

Often, getting caught doing something wrong teaches all that is necessary. By starting with a nonverbal response or by providing your child with a face-saving out, you can determine whether it is possible to move on without needing to say anything at all.

Offer your child an early way out of conflict by responding first with a knowing look, a step toward her, or a signal that says, "I caught you; this is enough; let it go." Then walk away with the assumption that nothing more needs to be said.

You can also defuse a pending conflict with a smile and a clever comeback that communicates, "I hear you, and I'm not buying into this."

"Nice try."

"Probably."

"That's a possibility."

"Could be."

"Thanks for sharing."

"What's your best guess as to what I'm about to do now?"

Finally, suggest an action that will get your child out of the conflict. Describe directly to your child the best way for her to walk out of the conflict if, at this point, she chooses to:

"Now is the time to set it down on the table and go back to your room."

"Close your mouth and walk away right now."

Once caught, many children want out of a confrontation but are unable to focus on how to get out. When your suggestion describes a path out without losing face, more often than not it will be taken. To a caught and scared child, a handy suggestion can be very persuasive.

You can also offer an out by acting as if the conflict were already over and you have moved on:

"You usually have better judgment than that. Let's get back to work."

"We don't need to talk about that do we?"

"I'm glad we got through that. Let's move on."

Stepping away from the situation, away from the power struggle, you provide the child with an opportunity to withdraw from the conflict without feeling that she has lost.

Be prepared with a comeback

Take a minute to practice the following comebacks as you imagine your child saying something that usually gets you going. Repeat each aloud with warmth and humor in your voice rather than sarcasm.

Nice try.

Probably.

That's a possibility.

Could be.

Thanks for sharing.

What's your best guess as to what I'm about to do now?

Think of one comment you might hear from your child soon:

_____

_____

Which comeback will you use to defuse the situation?

_____

_____

Forewarn and rehearse

The best time to deal with a child's anger is before the child gets angry. Once your child becomes angry, you don't have the luxury of going back in time, but you do have the opportunity to think of how to prevent the problem from happening again in the same way.

Often a child's anger is in response to being told to do something without enough warning—being suddenly told that it is time to go to bed or take a bath or come in from outside. If that is true for your child, provide him the extra time he needs by forewarning of any changes or demands ahead:

"Five minutes before you have to clean up."

"Two-minute warning."

You can also forewarn by rehearsing situations that evoke anxiety in the child. With practice, she will not be surprised, and she'll be more able to handle a difficult situation:

"Kari is probably going to want to play with your new toy. What can you say to her?"

"We have had a problem with bathroom time in the morning. Let's brainstorm some ideas."

Forewarning of change and rehearsing stressful situations before they happen will stop many angry outbursts before they occur. Here are several examples of forewarning:

"You know your grandmother will want to kiss you on the cheek. You need to decide if you can just let her or if you will ask her not to this time. Tell me what you have decided before she arrives."

"In the store, we will be walking by the game area. You know that we will not be buying anything today, right? Will you be able to walk by without getting upset?"

"In five minutes, you will need to turn off the computer. Pick out one thing you can be sure to finish in that amount of time."

Plan to forewarn

Think of a situation in your home that often turns into a problem:

_____

_____

Plan ahead this time in order to avoid the problem. What could you say to help your child be better prepared? Would a five-minute warning help? If so, what would that sound like?

_____

_____

Would it help to have the child rehearse what he is going to do so he is prepared? Do you need to offer a suggestion? If so, what would that be?

_____

_____

If nothing comes to your mind, ask your child for suggestions as to how you can help him deal with the situation. He may know exactly what would be helpful.

Handling Sibling Battles

To rebuild a cooperative sibling relationship, you need to treat your children like a team. With clear guidelines and expectations, you can use sibling conflict as an opportunity to teach your children the problem solving skills they will need in future relationships.

Make them a team

"She took my colored pencils and won't give them back."

"He always hides them so I can't find them."

Now if you want to, you can dive in, ask, "Who started this?" impose a solution and probably end up with both children angry at you.

Or you can use sibling conflict as the ideal opportunity to teach your children how to come up with their own solutions. Turn them into a team and assign them to solve the problem. In this way, you teach your children that it doesn't matter who is most to blame; since both are affected by the conflict, together they must arrive at a solution.

First, state your expectation of them in this situation:

"You two are old enough to share without fighting."

This positive expectation states the goal—your expectation of what should take place.

Then turn them into a team and give them the assignment.

"This problem belongs to both of you; together you need to come up with a plan to share the pencils without fighting."

Finally, commit to oversee the process.

"I'll stay until you have an idea you can try."

Creative problem solving

Teaching children this approach to problem solving—we have a problem, and we need to find a solution—encourages creative problem solving. It also discourages children from immediately looking for an adult to intervene.

By agreeing to oversee the process, you also make a commitment to "we-thinking."

"Talk together about possible solutions tonight, and we will discuss them at breakfast."

More often than not, long before the next morning, a solution will be in place. Learning to effectively resolve conflicts between siblings is particularly important because, unlike friends, siblings are forever—and conflict will remain until resolved. Making siblings a team, responsible for coming up with their own solutions, teaches skills of conflict resolution, skills they can use throughout their lives.

Stating your expectations may be done in some of the following ways.

"Twelve-year-olds can share without fighting."

"Doing chores together doesn't need to be unpleasant."

"You can play together without fighting over rules."

"Siblings don't need to fight over the TV."

These positive statements set the tone and direction for the team meeting you are requiring. It is best not to presume personal feelings that may not be there at the moment, such as, "I know you both love each other and don't want to see the other person hurt." At the moment, they may not feel loving, and they probably do want to see their sibling hurt. So better to keep it impersonal: "You can resolve this without fighting."

If your children are younger or need more direction, you can provide instructions that are more specific:

"Decide who plays with this toy at what time this afternoon."

"What is one thing you can both do to avoid this fight tomorrow?"

"Both of you call two friends and find out what rules they have about borrowing clothes in their homes."

Your involvement may be to sit with them until they come up with a solution. Or to check up on them later in the day. Or to arrange a time later for them to get together if now is not the time.

By staying involved from the sidelines, you demonstrate that their problem affects you, as well, and show your commitment to resolution.

Model conflict resolution with "we-thinking"

In any difficulty, particularly one with your partner, you have the opportunity to move beyond blaming and criticizing:" You never do anything for the kids in the evening," to defining the problem as a shared concern—"We have a problem and we need to find a solution."

"We need a better way to get the kids to school in the morning."

"How can we . . . ?"

"We-thinking" a problem begins with your acceptance that no matter who is wrong or who is to blame, the problem affects both of you. Resolving it together models conflict resolution for your children.

"This is causing a problem for us every morning."

Step closer. Increase communication rather than cutting it off. Meet when you can comfortably discuss the problem.

"Let's talk about it tonight, after the kids go to sleep."

Set aside distractions and listen to what the other person has to say. Express confidence that resolution can be found and welcome the opportunity this problem presents to improve yuor relationship.

"Let's take a minute to say what we need to say, then I'm sure we can come up with a better way. We always do once we have a chance to talk."

Then brainstorm better ways. Any concern that involves two people can be best approached with "we-thinking."

Practice finding solutions with your partner

What problem do you and your partner face?

_____

_____

What can you say to your partner to begin the "we thinking" process?

_____

_____

_____

Separate without blame

The most common response to sibling conflict, "Who started this?" is also the least productive. By attempting to find one child "right" and the other "wrong" you only encourage sibling rivalry. Whoever gets blamed this time will immediately start thinking of how to get back at the other one.

Most often, both children are to blame. Both were involved in some way. When that is true, it may simply be time for the children to be away from each other. Without any discussion of who was responsible, it is time to direct each to an activity that can be done alone.

Children need their own space, their own special possessions, and their own time alone. Often sibling conflict stems from siblings being thrown together too much or for too long. When conflict arises, time apart may, in itself, provide a cure.

"You two have played together enough. Josie, I need you to help me with the laundry. Kari, it's time to go outside for a while."

While this may not directly address the concern of the moment, it will create a break. Later you can talk to both children about what was taking place. Or, better yet, you can discuss it together when each child is more open to thinking about how to resolve the problem not just about who started it this time.

Timing is essential

Trying to get two angry, frustrated children to discuss solutions can be almost impossible. In any effort to resolve conflict, timing is a powerful tool. Resolution only comes about when you are all calm enough and strong enough to listen.

First consider whether it is best to address the conflict immediately or after a cooling off period If you and both children are calm, nondefensive, and accepting of criticism, dealing with a problem immediately may be best. If this is not the way you all feel, negotiate a cooling-off period instead. Separate the children and step away from the situation and the children for a time—however brief.

Then carefully select the time and place to discuss the concern. Choose a location that ensures you won't be interrupted, that feels safe for all of you, and that conveys the sense of intimacy or authority you believe will be most helpful to resolve the problem.

Planning the best time to address problems is an essential skill in effective conflict resolution. Modeling this for your children is the best way for them to learn that to be heard, you must speak when others are willing to listen.

Choose the right time

Make a list of the times that your children seem to have most difficulty getting along.

Next to each item, write a few words to describe the circumstances of that activity. Consider:

• how long they have been together beforehand
• how long the activity lasts
• if it involves one child getting her way more than the other
• who is best at or most enjoys the activity.

Activity	Circumstances
_____	_____
_____	_____
_____	_____
_____	_____

_____   _____

_____   _____

_____   _____

Select one of the activities on your list to work on first:

_____

What change could you make in the activity that might make it easier for your children to manage this time together?

• a shorter amount of time
• separate activities
• a break halfway through
• the involvement of other children

What change do you think would make it more workable for your children?

_____

_____

Reduce competition by speaking directly

"You clean up much better than your older sister," may seem like a good way to get older sister in line, but pointing out one child's good behavior to manipulate another child will usually backfire. "Look how well Shayna is putting away her clothes," is sure to leave the other child resentful and Shayna feeling used.

Whenever you say something to one child in the hope that another child will hear, you encourage sibling rivalry. Better to speak directly to the child whose behavior needs to change and to speak without making comparisons:

"Your side of the room needs to be picked up completely before you can invite a friend over this evening."

We also inadvertently encourage conflict when our praise of one child has a discouraging effect upon another child:

"Tyler is the family computer expert," can discourage other children who think they, too, know a lot about computers. Rather than praise a child in comparison to others in the family, simply praise him in his own right.

"Tyler has learned a lot about computers in the last year."

Praise and correction can be given without needlessly inviting sibling rivalry, by simply addressing only one child at a time:

"Once you clean underneath your bed, you are finished."

"It should be easy for you to find things in your closet now."

"Tyler's favorite subject is insects. Jason likes fire trucks."

Directing your comments to only one child at a time is the best way to ensure that your praise is not contributing to sibling conflict. Repeat these words of praise aloud or to yourself, substituting your child's name:

Instead of "Carl is the friendliest boy in the family," say, "Carl enjoys making friends."

Instead of "Janice is a much better reader than her sisters," say, "Janice enjoys reading and does it very well."

Continue with the following praises, substituting your child's name:

Yes, _____ stands up for herself at school.

Yes, _____ you are a lot of fun to be with.

Yes, _____ you have learned a lot this year.

Eliminate comparisons in your home

What is one thing you say in your home that inadvertently compares one child to another?

_____

_____

Write an alternative that speaks only to or about one child at a time.

_____

_____

Practice saying your new noncomparative sentence so it can come out automatically when you need it.

Give hope for new privileges

Treating your children absolutely equally won't guarantee that sibling rivalry will end. Sibling rivalry is natural, and cutting every cookie exactly in half will not correct it. When there are clear reasons for differing expectations, state them, showing that you can love both children in similar but not identical ways.

Most often, younger children seek what older children have. Rely on the differences in age to explain differences in expectations. Give hope to younger children that their time will come, and tell them when that will be:

"Your ten-year-old brother can go out alone. And when you are ten, you will be able to, also."

"Five-year-olds don't use a knife to carve wood. But when you get to be seven, you can start to carve if you show me then that you can be careful."

"Yes, your older sister picks out her own clothes. When you earn your own money, you can buy clothes on your own as well."

Other times, the older child resents the younger child's privileges:

"I didn't have a Nintendo when I was five. Why does he get one?"

Remind older siblings that younger children have had opportunities to learn from their older brothers and sisters. For this reason, responsibilities and privileges often do come earlier to younger children, something older children can take pride in.

"Yes, you didn't use carving tools alone until you were seven, but your younger sister has watched you use them carefully for years and has learned enough to begin at six. You have taught her well."

Differences in age expectations are best presented as a challenge to younger children and as an honor to older children.

Explain differences in siblings' privileges

What privilege does your younger child want that you are not ready to give?

_____

_____

Explain the rule and offer hope for the future:

_____

_____

What privilege does your younger child have that an older child resents?

_____

_____

Explain this in a way that honors the older child's contribution:

_____

_____

Develop borrowing rules

Labeling family and personal belongings can go a long way toward reducing one common source of sibling conflict.

Determine which toys, games, and clothing belong to the family and which belong to individuals. Decide on the rules for one family member using another family member's personal possessions:

"This book is Tana's, it was a gift for her last birthday. You need to ask for her permission to read it."

For family possessions, there need to be rules that are understood by all. Is it "first come first served" or "youngest selects" or "oldest has priority" or "share or you both lose it?"

The family also needs to develop and understand the rules that govern the family items that are in greatest demand:

"The family owns the TV. You two need to agree on both programs, or else you select the first and she the second half-hour. If you can't decide, the TV goes off."

Establish rules for borrowing as well. Identify which items can be borrowed and under what circumstances. Remember to include rules for borrowing when the person who owns an item is not home or is not available to be asked for permission.

Everyone also needs to understand what is expected when a borrowed object is damaged or lost. As in any contract, these things should be spelled out beforehand to avoid misunderstandings later.

Brainstorm solutions with your children

In your home, what items are fought over most?

_____

_____

When could you sit down with everyone involved and come up with a plan to reduce the fighting?

_____

_____

You might begin by asking if the children agree that there is a problem. Next, brainstorm solutions. If the children are older, listen to all of their ideas first, since they probably know the situation best. Select a plan, discuss any difficulties that might arise, and then schedule a time to get back together to see how well the plan is working.

Keep conflict specific and nonthreatening

There are effective ways to discuss a problem and there are damaging, hurtful ways. When kids are arguing, it's the perfect time to teach them about fair fighting just as you might remind them of the rules of any similar "competitive sport."

Even in the heat of a volatile exchange, you can step in and keep the discussion focused on a specific complaint rather than letting it degrade to a free-for-all. Teach your children to discuss one problem at a time:

"Your discussion is about whose turn it is to do the dishes. What happened last summer needs to be discussed another time. Stay on track and you can get this resolved."

Teach your children to listen and acknowledge each other's perspective even if they do not agree with it. Demonstrate that feeding back what you think the other person said helps to avoid misunderstanding.

"If you understand why s\he thought the jacket wasn't damaged, it would be helpful if you told her that before you continue."

"Did you hear your brother say that the jacket was fine when he picked it up?"

By keeping the discussion to one topic and acknowledging the other's perspective, you teach children to focus on resolution.

Finally, teach them that threats and insults will be punished; you will step in and impose a solution. In this way you ensure that any sibling discussion that takes place in front of you will stay civil and under control:

"Unless you stop calling each other names, I will remove the computer from your room, and that will end the discussion."

Episodes of sibling conflict provide an opportunity to teach your children healthy disagreement. They have a right to disagree but not in a hurtful, destructive way that violates the rules and expectations of your home.

Help your children identify destructive words

Sit down with your children and decide on family rules for arguments.

List the insults or threats that have been made in the past and are no longer allowed. Swear words that have been used in anger can be written down as well. This list can also include personal attacks that each child is particularly sensitive to.

_____

_____

_____

_____

_____

_____

Making this list may not seem productive, but writing down the insults children hurl at each other tends to take away the destructive power of the words. When words that hurt are discussed openly, children can acknowledge their choice to use or not use them and can recognize the power they have to make disagreements productive or destructive.

Focus on friendly resolution

When kids are arguing, the "rules of fairness" apply. You can expand those rules one step further by introducing the goal of ending disagreements with a friendly resolution. To achieve that, your children must learn to interrupt themselves when their words become too harsh.

Even in the heat of conflict you can step in to teach children the value of interrupting an argument to describe what they are feeling or seeing. You can also interrupt to state what you are feeling about what is taking place:

"This discussion is going nowhere."

"I'm getting tired of hearing you say the same thing over and over."

Teach them to interject humor or to briefly distract each other with something pleasant. Laughter helps people think more broadly, associate more freely, and notice relationships between people, events and circumstances that may have eluded them.

"Let's go get a bite to eat so we don't run out of steam before midnight. This argument is just getting good!"

Teach them to apologize for anything that has been done or said that continues to make resolution difficult.

"I'm sorry I called you obnoxious. I just didn't think you were listening to what I was saying."

Teaching children to interrupt an argument, to describe what they are feeling, to interject humor, and to apologize gives them the skills to move an argument from anger to resolution. They learn that interruption can redirect a discussion toward friendly resolution rather than spiraling destruction.

Keep discussions under control

Here are some other phrases that you can practice to keep a discussion from getting out of control: repeat each aloud:

"What is one thing you could have done to avoid this problem?"

"What do you need to be able to let this go? "

"Tell me what you think your brother is upset about?"

"It would help if you apologized for that last remark."

"Think you two can finish this before the end of the month?"

"You two simply disagree about this. Time to move on."

What do your children argue about regularly?

_____

_____

How could you help them describe what they are feeling?

_____

_____

How could you help them inject humor into a tense situation?

_____

_____

How could you encourage them to move on?

_____

_____

Initiate discussion during peaceful times

When you know your children are having difficulties, initiate discussion before the problems become unmanageable. Initiate the discussion yourself rather than waiting for the kids to open it for you. Lead off with your best guess:

"You're angry about what your sister said at the table last night, aren't you?"

Opening with a guess is more likely to get a response than by asking, "What's wrong with you?" or "What's your problem?" or even "What's the problem?" Accusative questions like these fail because they place the burden of disclosure upon the other person. Instead, try asking:

"Are you angry that your brother calls you names at school?"

Lay out how you perceive the problem. Describe what you are seeing, hearing, or feeling:

"It seems to me that you two are trying to make each other angry."

Guess at the emotion your child might otherwise find difficult to describe.

"Are you upset with Dana for not playing with you?"

If your guess is wrong, your child will correct you:

"No, I'm not upset, I'm just bored."

If your guess is right, however, you can go immediately to the heart of the discussion.

"Yes, I'm upset that she only wants to play her games and we never play what I want."

Opening a conversation by guessing at the problem and the emotions your children are struggling with will take you to the heart of the conflict before it escalates.

Here are additional examples of how to lead the way to discussion. Repeat each aloud or to yourself:

"You seem upset. Are you angry about what I said last night?"

"You must be hurt. Can you tell me what you happened?"

"You look discouraged. What were you hoping for?"

"Are you disappointed with the results?"

"You look frustrated. What are you having difficulty with?"

By suggesting an underlying emotion, you give your child both the opportunity and the words to describe in more detail what she is feeling and how you might be able to help her with that feeling.

Initiate a discussion with your child

Describe several recent incidents during which your child became angry or withdrawn. Beside each item, write the emotion that you think your child was feeling. Go beyond the words "angry" or "upset" to more specific feelings: hurt, disappointed, frustrated, jealous, envious, overwhelmed:

Incident	Feelings
_____	_____
_____	_____
_____	_____
_____	_____

Put your guess in the form of a question that will open a discussion:

_____

_____

Starting Over When All Else Fails

When conflict has gone on too long and both you and your child are discouraged, you need new insights and strategies to rebuild the trust and respect that have been strained.

Build an image to keep yourself positive

In the face of ongoing misbehavior, it can be difficult to believe that times ever were better or ever will be better again. The frustration of the moment can drain the strength you need to reach out one more time with patience and hope. To help yourself stay positive, build an image you can bring to mind—in even the most difficult moments— an image of the inherent worth of your child that can get you past the frustration of the moment.

Build this image during a quiet time, perhaps early in the morning. Recall favorite moments from your child's early years that never fail to bring a smile to your face. Add to this image at least one or two moments from recent months when you felt the joy of raising your child.

Then build a vision of your child at twenty-five or thirty-five years of age, a successful survivor, seated beside you as together you recall all that he or she put you through during these difficult years. Now add to this image your most imaginative, positive description of the qualities that now anger you most but that will someday to put to good use when your child is a successful lawyer, business person, or stand-up comedian.

Consider your child's similarities to you. Remember what you were like as a child and how, in time, you grew beyond your own childhood struggles.

Finally, remind yourself of the importance of your child to others, to friends or other adults who enjoy your child's best moments while you deal with the more difficult ones.

Now blend this collage of images and develop a phrase that you can repeat to yourself instantly when difficulties arise:

"He's just practicing to be a great lawyer so he can support me in my old age."

"This persistence is perfect for college."

"He's just like me; I made it, and so will he."

When you are at the edge—in danger of creating long-term harm to your relationship with destructive words or impulsive reactions— let this image and phrase jump to your mind to prompt the strength you need to be creative and caring one more time.

Courage for the moment

Draw from the past and reach to the future for the courage you need to get you through the moment.

As you create a collage in your mind of past and future successes, you can also create a collage on the wall. With your child (though you could do it alone), create a collage of images on poster board that recall your child's best moments and future dreams. Include photos, souvenirs, notes from teachers, awards, or favorite drawings. Jot down a friend's name or a one-word reminder of a trip or an afternoon adventure. Add to the collage images of what your child hopes to be. If she dreams of being a pilot, cut out a picture of a pilot from a magazine. If he wants to be a rock star, find a picture of his favorite musician.

Fill the collage with dreams, then let it be a reminder to both of you of the best of the past and your hopes for the future. Place it prominently in your home, not necessarily in your child's bedroom. When you and your child are lost in the drama of a difficult moment, this collage can be the passage backward and beyond—an escape to better times. Add to the collage as often as possible, expanding it as needed.

Create a positive image of your child

Recall incidents from your child's earlier years that can always bring a smile to your face. Quickly jot one-word reminders:

_____

_____

Now envision your child at twenty-five or thirty-five. Imagine sitting together and laughing at the difficulties you are having at this moment. Jot down where this conversation might take place, what you each look like, and what you might say:

_____

_____

In what way is your child most like you? One word:

_____

What is the most positive description you can give to the qualities that now anger you most? Is your child particularly persistent, assertive, creative, expressive? In what situation or profession is that quality considered a strength? Write the quality and the profession it serves best:

_____

_____

Consider the importance of your child to others, to his or her friends. Do other adults see positive qualities in your child that sometimes escape your eyes? What do others enjoy about your child?

_____

_____

Hold these thoughts and these images in your mind. As you gather them, write down a single phrase or sentence that can bring these thoughts to mind at a difficult time:

_____

_____

Remain the adult

Have you ever felt the urge to retaliate with defensive, childlike behavior when frustrated or angry with your child—to treat your child exactly as she treats you? If you were both children, that would be fair—to treat her as she treats you. But you're not.

It is a child's job is to act like a child—to rebel, test limits, try out new words, explore the limits of anger, assert herself, and in so doing, discover who she is.

As a child that was your job. But your job now is to be an adult. Uncontrolled anger, name-calling, insults, and demeaning comments are not adult behaviors.

No matter what she says or does to you, your job—and it is not easy—is to model the respect you expect someday to see in return. No matter how strong the urge, name-calling—"You're nothing but a brat," insults—Can't you do anything right?" and ridicule—"Is the little bitty baby's tantrum over now?" only reveal the child in you. You can be decisive without being threatening, firm without being abusively loud. That's what a child needs to see from an adult.

Adults may show frustration and anger but never hatred toward a child. An adult maintains perspective and humor, gives attention when needed not just when convenient, and stays with a problem until it is resolved. Your responsibility as an adult is to be what you ask your child to be—willing to listen, to change your opinion, and to own up when you are wrong.

Although you can tell your children what to do, they will most likely become what you *are*, not what you *say*. To turn around a troubled relationship, be sure, first, that you are modeling the qualities you want your child to value and display.

Prepare to model adult behavior

When all else fails and the distance between you and your child grows greater, think of the qualities or virtues you value but find it difficult to display. Patience? Understanding? Acceptance? Forgiveness? Firmness? Consistency?

_____

_____

Now think of a specific situation during which it would be extremely difficult for you to display one or more of these qualities:

_____

_____

What would you have to say or do or not do to to help your child see those qualities in you? Be as specific as possible:

_____

_____

_____

Before this situation occurs again, make an opportunity to practice this response. You might say the words to yourself or sit quietly and visualize yourself acting in the way you would like to. Imagine, as well, the response you would like from your child. It may not be there at first, but it is important to have an idea of the effect you would like your response to have on your child

Then give a try. Although your child may not immediately respond as you hope, at least you are acting in the way you would like your child to act.

Choose your timing wisely

Wouldn't it be wonderful if you could choose when your child will misbehave. You might say, "OK, you can kick someone if you must, but not my boss and not someone bigger than I am." Of course, you can't choose the timing of misbehavior. But you do have more power over when and how to deal with it than you might think.

The heat of the moment is not usually the best time to deal with a problem. An upset, crying child is seldom able to profit from all the wonderful insights you have on what she should have done.

You have the power to wait—to give yourself a few minutes to think—before you once again ground her for the next three years. "We'll deal with this later," gives your child plenty of time to imagine what you're going to say. Delay will also help you decide what is worth dealing with and what is not worth more attention.

Admonish in private

When you and your child are both calm enough to talk, admonish her in private. Make it short, direct, restate your love, and move on:

"Hitting me is not acceptable. I love you, and I'll stop whatever I am doing to listen when I see that you are upset. But hitting me is not OK."

A verbal response from the child would be great, but it is not always necessary.

Once you have said what you needed to say, distance is no longer needed. Comfort your child if your words have upset her or your anger has scared her, and save additional comments for another time when she is again calm enough to listen.

Powerful moments

In every relationship, there are powerful moments—occasions when criticism is most likely to be listened to. In your home, it might be at bedtime, early in the morning, or during a walk. Bring up difficult matters during these magical times when real change can happen:

"I have something I need to discuss. Let's take a short walk before your sister arrives."

If your child has trouble with the intensity of being corrected, it may be best to bring up a problem when he is occupied with an activity. Some children listen best when their hands and eyes are busy. Asking your child to look at you while you reprimand him is not necessary.

Misbehavior occurs at the most inconvenient times. Say and do what is needed to move on at the moment, then save the real conversation for a time when you both feel powerful—when you are in control of what you need to say and your child feels strong enough to hear it.

The wise use of timing is one of the most important tools you have in turning around a relationship.

Find the powerful moments

If your relationship with your child is strained, it's especially important to find times that he will be willing to talk with you. At what time or during what activity would that be most likely to happen?

_____

_____

If it's been a long time since you've talked calmly and respectfully with each other, think back to past years when your relationship was better and recall an activity that you enjoyed doing together:

_____

How could you encourage your child to again join you in that activity?

_____

_____

Is there a new activity that you might participate in and in doing so find a way to connect with your child?

_____

_____

Create small successes
to empower change

Misbehavior—hitting when angry, for example—may be all that your
child knows how to do or has ever done in a specific situation. Learning a new way to behave—to walk away and tell you she is upset—may
be difficult. How can you help your child feel strong enough to make
the change you are asking of her?

Encourage feelings of strength and confidence

First, consider the situations in which your child feels capable. How
can you create more opportunities for her to experience feelings of com-
petence, growth, and change?

Next consider the people who care for her. We all, even early in life,
have people who inspire us, people who help us feel good about ourselves. You are surely one of those people for your child, but there are
others also. Can you arrange for additional time with your child's supportive friends.

Finally, build strength in your child by being the historian of her
best moments and finest intentions.

"Remember when you buckled down for three hours that afternoon and finished the report just in time."

Express amazement at all that is inconsistent with your child's best
intentions:

"It surprises me this is bothering you so much. Usually you ignore
name-calling."

And display confidence in her ability:

"You'll be able to handle this. You have in the past and you will today."

To make a behavior change requires strength and confidence. To turn a relationship around, create opportunities for your child to draw strength from what she does well, from people she enjoys, and from your reminders of all she has done well in the past.

Help your child feel strong enough and confident enough to change

Sometimes the path to behavior change is indirect. Any activity that increases your child's belief in himself will make him more receptive to the changes you request because he will believe that he can make them.

Jot one word reminders to the following questions.

What activities does your child do well?

_____

_____

To build his confidence and his belief in his ability to change, what can you do to create more occasions for these activities?

_____

_____

What is a new activity you could introduce with the sole intention of increasing his confidence in himself?

_____

_____

List the people with whom your child has connected well—neighbors, relatives, and friends:

_____

_____

When your child is struggling, how could create or encourage additional time with these people?

_____

_____

Every relationship has an occasional need for a third party to step in and help bridge difficulties. An old friend may be able to discuss a concern with your child and create the new start you are looking for.

Rebuild relationships

Why do children do what we ask them to do? They respond because they value their relationship with us. If that relationship deteriorates, becoming stressful, punitive, and no longer loving, misbehavior may become more appealing than cooperation.

When the ties that bind your relationship become too frayed, children have uniquely effective ways of ignoring you or refusing to do what you ask of them. Most of their strategies can be referred to as misbehavior. If you don't have time to strengthen your relationship with your child, discipline strategies will not be effective.

You can measure the need for increased time together by assessing the level of problems that now exist; then consider the time you spend together and the amount of positive attention you have given recently. Ask yourself: Do I need to give more of myself in order to get the change in behavior that I seek, or do we just need to spend our time together more wisely?

Make time for your child

Could you increase the time you spend together, staying home one more evening each week or joining your child for lunch? Even an extra half hour can help.

Create extended uninterrupted times together by sharing tasks such as folding the laundry, raking leaves, or painting a room. Or do whatever your the child suggests. It's important to give attention when it's most needed. If your child most wants time with you when you first get home from work, schedule it. It's important. If your children battle for your attention while you're trying to read the mail after work , consider changing the order in which you do things. When you get home, go immediately to your children for ten minutes, play and listen to all they have to tell you, then share stories with your partner, and only later check the mail. That's likely to reduce the daily fight for your attention.

By giving more time, planning for uninterrupted time, and giving time when your child most needs it, you begin the rebuilding process that is essential for turning around a difficult relationship.

Make the most of brief moments

Since you probably don't have more time today than you did yesterday, the trick is to make the most of small moments. Turn insignificant amounts of time into special moments by giving your child your full attention without allowing your mind to be on other concerns.

What do you talk about while in the car together? What might your child enjoy doing or talking about during travel time?

Is there time to talk in the morning, even in the bathroom or while you are getting dressed?

Could you call your child during lunch hour or occasionally join him at school for lunch?

Are you available at bedtime? Could you leave a note in the morning before you leave for work or call before the children leave for school?

Any time during the day that you are with your child can yield special moments as long as you focus on your child and avoid thinking about other issues and problems.

Turn time together into good times

On the chart on the following page, list the daily activities you do with your child along with the times in minutes. This may be a surprisingly long or disturbingly short list.

Minutes   Activity

_____   _____

_____   _____

_____   _____

_____   _____

_____   _____

_____   _____

_____   _____

_____   _____

_____   _____

_____   _____

After you make the list, put a check next to the activities that sometimes have a special quality to them—times when, in the past, you have connected enjoyably with your child.

What is one thing you might do, or talk about, or ask your child about the next time you participate in this activity together.

_____

Consider starting a entertainment tradition during times you are together—maybe math games in the car or riddles in the laundry room or story telling while doing dishes. Traditions are easy to start, you just begin. What traditions could you begin in your home this week to turn a dull, insignificant time into a time you enjoy sharing together?

_____

_____

_____

Determine to be more creative

Ask yourself, "If I were my child, what would it really take for me to want to change?"

To turn around a struggling relationship with your child, your approach needs to be bold and daring. Continuing to do the same old things will further frustrate both of you. You must dare to try; you must dare to fail.

Children who believe that they cannot change become very skilled at convincing other that they will not change. They may, in fact, want desperately to change but not know how or where to begin.

Do the unexpected . . . do the opposite.

If you always get angry when he doesn't take his plate to the sink after dinner, next time laugh.

"I really thought for a moment you were going to pick that up and carry it to the kitchen. Joke's on me."

Or make a point to carry it out yourself:

"Here, I'll take care of it. You just sit down and relax."

If you have been doing the same thing every night for the last six months and nothing has changed, almost anything else you do has a better possibility of prompting a change.

Silence may be golden

Recognize when there is nothing more to be said and nothing more to be done for a time. Let silence convey your respect for your child's ability to learn on his own time and your willingness to be patient.

Don't reject any options

You must be willing consider all possibilities, even those you never thought you would ever have to face. There may even be exceptional circumstances that require an extreme intervention—psychiatric hospitalization for a disturbed teenager or a temporary move out of your home.

Consider creative interventions

Imagine yourself as your child. Consider all that you know about your child, his fears, likes, and dislikes.

———————————————————

———————————————————

Imagine that you are your child. What could your parents do that would make you want to change? List all the ideas that come to mind, whether sensible or ridiculous.

———————————————————

———————————————————

———————————————————

Consider each idea in turn. Even if you can't carry out your idea exactly as you imagined it, it may be feasible if modified. Where will you start?

———————————————————

———————————————————

Imagine the power of small changes

When problems are persistent and overwhelming, it is difficult to notice that your child is doing anything right. But if you feel overwhelmed, imagine how discouraged your child must feel. Somehow your child most find some way to believe that he can change and that he is changing already.

The greatest challenge in having a difficult child is to reward the small changes that are a step in the right direction but are still a long way from where you want the child to be.

If your child has always struck you when angry, yelling obscenities is a step forward. If that step is not acknowledged in some way, she will probably go back to hitting:

"I don't like that you are screaming those words at me, but you stopped yourself from hitting, and I appreciate that. You are learning to control yourself better."

Sometimes the image of change can't really be seen but needs to be imagined. If your child almost never takes a bath without a tantrum, the next time (provided he is not the worst he has ever been), say to him after his bath:

"That was better than usual. I can tell you are getting older."

State the improvement (even if you have to almost imagine it) and tie that improvement to something the child finds desirable (acting older).

"You're having fewer fights at the playground than you used to when you were younger. You must be learning to talk when you get upset instead of just hitting someone."

In these ways, you can help your child realize that he can change, that he is changing, and that the changes have been noticed and appreciated. It may be a long time before you see behavior that would normally be rewarded, but the only way to get there is to reward the small improvements along the way.

Imagine improvement

Think of a behavior in which your child seems very stuck; there has been little improvement in this behavior for a long time:

_____

_____

What you would like him to be doing?

_____

_____

Complete the following statements with the change you would like to see:

You are doing better _____

I've noticed you've been _____

It seems you are learning _____

You are getting better at _____

Make those positive affirmations to your child whenever you see even a hint of improvement. To be effective there must be some evidence of positive change; although it may be very little. The improvement you are stating must sound 2 percent believable—or at least not absolutely ridiculous. But at some point, bringing your child's attention to a 2 percent improvement will be more useful than continuing to pound on the 98 percent failure.

Choose your battles with care

When struggles seem only to lead to new struggles, it's time to step in and look at what you are fighting over and what is no longer worth the battle. Consider the things you battle over with your child. Think of the big struggles and then of the smaller struggles, as well.

Can you let go for now?

In order to move the relationship forward, what are you willing to let go of? If your child is failing in school, does it matter at the moment what her room looks like? Are table manners a priority when she is threatening to run away from home? If you want her to express her anger in words, are you willing to accept the words she chooses even if you don't like them?

It may be time to determine and focus on high priorities, ignoring less important issues that will probably resolve themselves eventually. Focus on the moment. What is important today? Direct all of your attention to resolving the most important conflict or solving the most serious problem.

Let go of a daily battle

Select one daily battle that may not be worth the struggle and that you may be willing to let go of:

_____

_____

If a neighbor child did this would you say anything?

_____

Is your response is useful or is it only building walls between you and your child?

_____

Is your concern about this issue more helpful or more harmful at this time?

_____

Are you asking your child to be someone she isn't?

_____

Will this issue matter next week, next month, or next year? If it will, could it be resolved then?

_____

If your answers to the questions above tell you to let go of this battle, what will you say to remind yourself of this decision?

_____

_____

Building Responsible Individuals

Develop parenting skills that encourage wise decision making and responsible behavior in your children. Teach them to become confident and to take action.

Invite early into family decision making

Traditionally, many Native American children are allowed to participate in important family and tribal discussions at a very young age,
shortly after they learn to talk. In this way, children learn two important things: first, that there is a place for their opinion, and second, that
their opinion is only one of many. Your children will enjoy being involved as well, learning early that their opinions will be listened to and
valued. It will be important, however, to distinguish between when you
are asking for family input and when your decision already has been
made.

Teach decision making skills

When you involve children in a decision, teach the skills of good decision making. First discuss the problem and the need for a solution.
Second, brainstorm possible solutions. Third, select the single best option. Finally, schedule a time to review progress.

These four steps—discussion, brainstorming, selection, and review—present a model for personal problem solving that you can ask
your child to use whenever a problem arises.

"This is the third time this week we have gotten to school late. You
don't enjoy walking in late and it is annoying to your teacher as well.
(Clarify the problem and the need for a solution)

"What are some things we could do differently to help us leave the
house on time? (Brainstorm).

"We'll list possible solutions, select one, and review it next week at this time."

The four steps in problem solving

Step one: Clarify the problem. Identify what the difficulty is and how you feel about it.

Step two: Brainstorm. Accept and write down all ideas without evaluating them. No matter how outrageous an idea is, write it down. Evaluate ideas later, not as they are mentioned during brainstorming. If ideas get shot down as soon as they are offered, children will be hesitant to say anything.

Step three: Select the best option. Evaluate each idea, discussing its good and bad points. Imagine possible obstacles to success. Finally, choose the best option.

Step four: Implement the solution and set a time to review progress. Setting a time to review ensures that, if the first solution is unsuccessful, a new solution will be considered as soon as possible.

Practice problem solving

Consider one problem that is on your mind at this time.

Step one: Describe the problem and how it makes you feel?

_____

_____

Second: Brainstorm by writing down all possible solutions that come to mind, even the more outrageous.

_____

_____

_____

_____

_____

Third: consider each in turn. Which seems most likely to be successful?

_____

_____

Are there any obstacles to be overcome that you see already?

_____

_____

Fourth: when will give the solution a try, and when will you check in to evaluate it?

_____

_____

Release responsibility daily

As we watch children grow, it is easy to continue to do for them what they were long ago able to do for themselves. We continue because doing it ourselves is faster or easier or simply because we've done it since the child was born. Waiting for your child to tie her shoes can be a nerve wracking experience when you're running late. And it's easier to lay out a child's clothes than wait for the child to decide on a favorite outfit for the day.

But learning responsibility begins with these little tasks. And in these and almost every daily activity, a child's ability to accept greater responsibility increases monthly, weekly, and sometimes daily. It's just a question of whether we notice and provide opportunities for the child to try. Showing acceptance of your child's efforts to choose for himself is more important than which jacket the child wears on a specific day. A sudden cold wind teaches more than all the warnings a parent can give to "wear your winter jacket."

Making wise decisions is a skill. It requires practice, and it necessarily involves making mistakes on occasion. Like any skill it is best begun early and is learned most easily when presented in manageable steps.

Guide decisions

To help guide your child's decisions, you can be begin by offering choices that are acceptable to you. As a next step, ask questions to prompt your child's own evaluation. Finally allow your child to make and live with her own decisions.

Begin by offering two choices, either of which is acceptable to you:

"You can choose the blue jacket or the red jacket today."

When your child is comfortable making simple decisions, begin asking questions to prompt her evaluation of options:

"Which jacket do you think would be best on a cold day like today?"

When she begins making those decisions thoughtfully, allow her to make her own decisions.

You might occasionally offer your thoughts as guidance, provided you can do this without implying that only one choice will get your approval.

"That jacket isn't as warm as it looks, is it? But it is a good spring jacket."

Begin releasing responsibility to your child

Make a list of all the things you do for your child throughout one day.

_____

_____

_____

_____

_____

_____

_____

_____

Review the list and put a check next to tasks you think your child could probably do without any assistance at all.

Finally, determine how you will turn over responsibility. You might consider the following phrases. Repeat each aloud for practice:

I forget you can _____ by yourself.

You're probably now old enough to _____.

I bet you can _____ on your own.

I don't need to be _____ for you, do I?

Coach from the sidelines

Knowing when to listen, just listen, is one of the most valuable skills for a parent.

"I got in trouble for not getting an assignment done today."

Now you surely have innumerable lectures you could deliver at this point, or you could express interest with a simple "hmm" and wait to hear what follows.

"The work was too hard anyway, and I don't like the teacher."

Respond minimally, but not absently, at first. Say little but turn to give attention, so your minimal response isn't mistaken for disinterest. Because you didn't immediately charge your child with laziness, he told you what he sees as the problem—hard assignments and difficulty with the teacher.

Make a guess

To better understand what your child is feeling, make your best guess. You might say: "You sound discouraged." He might say: "Yeah, he made me stay in from recess for the second time this week." By rephrasing what your child is feeling, you show empathy without suggesting that you are going to solve the problem for him. Acknowledgment helps your child understand that what he feels is okay and that you have faith he can resolve it himself.

By asking questions, you can guide your child's thinking back to his ability to solve the problem on his own.

"What could you do to make a change?"

By not diving in immediately with your opinions and suggestions, you give your child an opportunity to take responsibility for finding his own solutions. Later, if needed, you can help him clarify the real issue that needs to be dealt with:

"Are you having trouble with the work or just finding it hard to get it done on time?"

Parents feel powerful when they have an immediate and wonderful solution to every problem their children face. But by providing children with the opportunity to develop their own solutions, personal responsibility grows.

Avoid platitudes

When you want to express concern or understanding, it is best to avoid simple platitudes that diminish the importance of what the child is feeling.

"No sense crying over spilled milk."

"Everyone makes mistakes."

"No one is perfect."

Respond with understanding, but without judgement.

"It is frustrating to lose something you like, isn't it?"

Your response will be more powerful if it comes from your experience rather than relying on trite phrases that trivialize your child's struggle. Repeat these aloud, if you'd like, to practice being personal in your response.

"I never liked being teased when I was a child either."

"This is going to take more practice, isn't it. I had a hard time sticking to a practice schedule."

"I don't think losing is easy for anyone; it wasn't for me." _____

Help your child find solutions

Next time your child comes to you with a problem that you believe she has the ability to figure out on her own, decide to respond with a minimal, "hmm." What problem might she bring to you in the next few days?

_____

_____

If she does bring the problem you are imagining at the moment, what is your best guess as to the feeling she would be experiencing when she tells you about this problem. Keep this word in mind, in case you have the opportunity to rephrase what she says to you.

_____

What can you say to help her to clarify what she is dealing with?

_____

_____

What can you say to help her to come up with her own solutions. Practice these openings:

"What have you done before that has worked?"

"What would you like to do?"

"How would another person handle this?

"What do you think would be the best thing for you to do now?"

Turn praise back on your child

We all enjoy praise, hearing that others like or admire what we have done. But seeking praise can become obsessive and debilitating, particularly when a child learns to value her work only when it pleases others. To avoid the down side of praise, turn the praise back on your child:

"You must be very happy to have created something so lovely." "You can be very proud of yourself."

If you do give your opinion, it will be more valued by your child if you speak to something specific. "Nice job" or "Good work," doesn't communicate the interest that a more specific comment would, such as:

"The colors of the mountains are very well done on this drawing."

"The chair is particularly well sketched."

Specific praise shows that you actually took the time to look closely and want to help your child recognize what, in your opinion, was most noteworthy.

You can also focus your comment on the child's efforts or emerging skill rather than directing your praise to one specific product.

"You are learning to be a marvelous artist."

"Your sketches are more detailed than last month."

But avoid exaggerated praise—praise that places an expectation upon the child that he knows he can not fulfill. "You are always the most generous boy," or "You will be the top of your class in math by the end of this year," may sound like praise, but the pressure can be too much for a child who knows he can't always be what you expect.

Practice praise

Think of something your child is likely to bring to you, expecting your praise or approval? What would he typically say to you?

_____

_____

Repeat the following openings, finishing with the example you just wrote and helping your child value his work himself.

You must be very proud of having

_____

"Did you ever imagine you would be able to

_____

Remember when you thought you would never

_____

Look how well you have learned to

_____

Who would you most like to tell about this?

Encourage critical thinking

You can build in your child the strength to seek more than the praise of others and to rise above the pressure to conform. You can encourage your child's ability to critically evaluate herself and the world in which she lives.

We evaluate ourselves honestly by developing the ability to look at our own behavior and notice the contradictions between how we act and how we wish we had acted. By encouraging children to look for lessons in their mistakes, they can begin this process of honest evaluation and can avoid being paralyzed by failure.

Your child can also be taught to recognize when a friend's actions are inconsistent with who that friend says he is. The skill of evaluation is best taught by asking questions rather than offering criticism.

"John was two hours late getting home from school yesterday and his mom was worried? What do you think about that?"

"Karen borrowed your jacket and returned it torn. How does that make you feel about your friendship?"

Teach children to be wise consumers

Learning to evaluate information and become wise to marketing strategies is another aspect of critical evaluation. The teaching can begin the first time your child realizes the toy he bought doesn't look as good or work as well as it did in the commercial he saw on television. At that point, you can begin to discuss such the ploys used to market toys deceptively. You can discuss advertising copy that presents a toy as the key to happiness or to making friends.

Compare prices of objects with designer names and equivalent products without the big names; then discuss whether there is a difference in quality or function or whether the only difference is in the association with a famous personality. This is best done as part of a general discussion not when your child is begging for a specific item.

Above all, you can demonstrate how your own critical evaluation guides what you buy for your child and for yourself.

Helping your child to develop critical thinking will encourage her to take greater responsibility for what she chooses to value and strive for in life.

Evaluate advertising

Poking holes in advertising claims can be a valuable exercise in critical thinking and a lot of fun as well. Begin with products other than toys so your child doesn't feel you are criticizing an item to avoid buying it. What product currently being advertised would provide a good beginning?

What questions can you ask to help your child make the evaluation?

_____

_____

_____

Where could you and your child find more information about this product?

_____

_____

After using this process to evaluate several products advertised to adults, encourage your child to begin analyzing toy ads in the same manner.

Build resilience
with nutrition and exercise

Building physical resilience is a key to building psychological resilience and to improving your child's ability to handle stress. Stress affects people of all ages, not just adults. It reduces their ability to concentrate and utilize intelligence. Stress, if not handled well, makes people, including children, less capable.

Developing and maintaining good health habits will give you and your children the strength you need to get through difficult times.

Important stress management skills

Develop good eating habits. No other factor is more instrumental in someone's physical resilience through the day. Discuss foods that build the body and those that only fill the stomach with empty calorie. Provide healthful foods rather than sugar- and fat-laden snack foods.

Enjoy exercise. Going for a run creates a high arousal state within the body and reduces feelings of sadness or discouragement. Vigorous exercise will build the physical reserves necessary to move through difficult times. Help your child explore a variety of physical activities until he finds several that he enjoys.

Teach the skill of relaxation. Relaxation is effective in confronting high-energy moods like anger or anxiety. Progressive muscle relaxation, breathing and stretching exercises, meditation, and biofeedback calm the spirit and renew the body.

Encourage supportive friendships A network of supportive friendship and relationships provides the key to confronting loneliness.

Build physical resilience in your children

Which resilience skills will be most important to the child you are concerned about? Make notes on what you can do to teach these skills.

Nutrition awareness? Is there a family history of weight problems or unhealthy eating habits? If so, now is the time to help your child with the information, suggestions or encouragement.

_____

_____

Exercise? Does he get enough physical exercise? If exercise is not a family habit, joining him in daily exercise of some type will help both of you to deal with your daily stresses.

_____

_____

Relaxation training? Does your child have difficulty settling down or falling asleep. Progressive muscle relaxation, deep breathing, or meditation skills will serve him well throughout her life.

_____

_____

Supportive friendships? Without the ability to make friends, the stresses of life can be overwhelming. If your child lacks this skill, speak to a school counselor or whoever might be able to teach your child how to make and keep friends. This is an important skill for lifelong happiness.

_____

Which one of these resilience skills—nutrition, exercise, relaxation or friendship—is most needed in your child's life?

_____

Teach the skill of optimism

People can be taught to develop optimism. Encourage your child to recognize that tomorrow can be different and that everyone can change. Help her to see failure as temporary, situational, and merely another challenge to be overcome. Teach her to forgive herself and others, recognizing that others struggle just as she does.

As you build a home that encourages empowerment, you place your child in an increasingly healthy, responsive, enlightening environment in which to continue learning and growing.

Creating a vision of positive change is crucial to any effective discipline program. As you help your child to be optimistic about the future, to believe that she can change, you make it possible for her to do so. Teaching the ability to grow and change and turn around past behavior is essential to the development of future possibilities.

Three ways to encourage optimism

Laughter is a critical component in building resistance to stress and in developing the resilience to bend rather than break. One major key to flexibility is to make laughter a fundamental skill in balancing your mood, your perspective, and your life. Laughter actually creates a physiological change, releasing endorphins that relieve pain and bringing about a return to overall balance throughout the body. As you model the sheer joy of laughter, your child will copy your behavior and will become more optimistic about life.

Maintaining healthy rituals is a way to appreciate the passage of time unencumbered by momentary disruptions. Some rituals must remain inviolable in order to tie people to the flow of their life. Spending a few minutes alone with your child at bedtime provides a reminder of your constant love. Special birthday dinners that mark growth and maturity can be especially important to a child struggling to improve his behavior and outlook.

Healthy risk-taking activities increase a child's confidence in his abilities and have been shown to increase the level of endorphins—hormones that counter depression. Encourage your child to accept challenges, to take measured risks, to not fear failure, and to enjoy success.

Encourage optimism in your child

If your child seems pessimistic about life, what does he say to indicate his lack of hope?

_____

_____

Without confronting his pessimism directly, how you could encourage a more optimistic view of life? How can you demonstrate and encourage free flowing laughter?

_____

_____

What rituals can you begin or restore that will help your child see hope beyond today's problems?

_____

_____

What activities would give your child confidence by providing a measured risk along with the possibility of success.

_____

_____

Nurture outside relationships

When seeking a path to long-term behavior change, search for solutions among friends, family, neighborhood, and community. Change is difficult. To have the strength to change, we reach out to others who believe in us. Often the most powerful and influential interactions in a child's world take place among his or her peers. Adult approval cannot completely substitute for positive peer relationships. The therapeutic value of peer relationships is particularly important and necessary to children who have learned to mistrust the advice and attention of adults. Peer friendships go a long way toward rebuilding a child's connection with his world.

How can you support your child's peer relationships? Are there clubs or organizations you can encourage your child to join in order to expand his friendships among both younger and older children? Often children who are having a difficult time with their peers show great patience when helping younger children. Consider children with whom your child already has a positive relationship. How can you encourage these friendships?

Children can be taught the value of reaching beyond the family for support through difficult times and can learn to take responsibility for maintaining contacts that make them feel good about themselves. Maintaining relationships beyond the family teaches children to take responsibility for building the support they may need to get through difficult times.

Does your child need help learning to get along with others? If so, consider the following sources of support:

A school group run by counselors

Boy or Girl Scouts

Youth groups connected with your religious community

Special interest groups such as chess clubs or musical groups

Sports organizations

If your child is having difficulty making friends, watch him with other children and try to understand what he needs to learn in order to get along better. Discuss this with the group leader or school counselor. Then consider a variety of ways to teach this skill. They may include enrolling him in a social skills classroom, providing counseling if that is available, or involving a sympathetic adult friend or an older child.

Create a support network

Whether your child has almost no friends, a few friends, or many, developing even more friendships is valuable.

What characteristics of your child may make it difficult for her to maintain friendships?

_____

_____

What groups might provide a structure for teaching your child the skills needed to make and keep friends?

_____

_____

If more help is needed, what adults or older children could provide guidance for your child?

_____

_____

Teach children to act not complain

You build responsible individuals when you teach children to act rather than complain.

Complaining comes naturally to most kids; they hear enough of it in their world to pick it up quite easily. But learning to take action when they want something to change is an attitude and skill that must be taught.

If you want something to change, you have to change something

When your child says that he wishes something was different, that is the time to step in and explore actions that could make change likely to happen.

Which circumstances are in your child's control? Help your child to see steps he could take on his own to create a change. If he complains that a friend borrows his videos and does not return them, teach him to say "no" clearly and firmly.

Who could help him create the change he seeks? If he is not able to create the change on his own, who is available to help him? Teach him that reaching out to others to meet his goal is another way to take responsibility to create change rather than merely complain. If school playground equipment isn't safe, talk with him about the people who must be told about the problem so repairs will be made: his teacher, the custodian, the principal. Then encourage him to go either alone or with friends to present the problem to the appropriate people.

Does change require a new attitude on his part? What help does your child need to examine his priorities and desires. Would counseling or a conversation with someone else who has been through what he is facing be helpful?

When you teach your child to take responsibility for the change he seeks, you provide an important life skill.

Teach your child to act

What complaint can you anticipate your child will make in the next week?

_____

_____

Which circumstances can he control? What questions could you ask to help him discover those circumstances?

_____

_____

Who could help him create the change he wants?

_____

_____

If the change requires a new attitude from him, who could help him make that change in attitude?

_____

Confronting the Stress of Parenting

Parenting is a twenty-four-hour job that you do best when you build in healthy routines, supportive friends, and reasonable expectations for both you and your child.

Exercise to become more resilient

Do you notice a difference between how you calmly you deal with your children at the start of the day and how much more difficult it can be when you come home tired at the end of the day?

Your ability to deal with difficult behavior is affected by how you feel physically. Taking steps throughout a busy day to increase your physical resilence may seem to be a low priority, but if you can steal five to twenty minutes for a walk, stretch, or brief workout, you'll have the strength to deal better with your children the remainder of the day.

The trick is to get exercise that is different from the typical running around you do with children. Here are some alternatives to consider.

Stretching increases circulation and works your muscles to build flexibility and resilience. Anytime you are standing, take a moment to bend forward, back, and to the sides. Then clasp your hands behind you and bend forward again. Stretching can also be done in bed, before you get up in the morning.

Shallow knee bends are also possible anytime you are standing. Or, while washing the dishes or standing in line, support yourself on a single leg, slightly bent, alternating from side to side.

Deep breathing is a classic relaxation technique. When anxious we tend to breathe shallowly. Instead, take time throughout the day to breathe deeply into your lower abdomen. Breathe in to a count of five then out to a count of five for a quick refresher at any time.

If you work on a computer or perform other repetitive tasks with your hands and arms, give them a quick massage. Begin with your inner forearm, move down to your palm, up each finger, down the back of your hand, then all the way back up your forearm.

Taking care your physical needs is essential to effective parenting. The demands on your time are tremendous, but so too are the demands on your body. Steal moments throughout the day to refresh yourself, for your own good and the good of those you care for.

A great quick energizer

When you don't have time for a walk or run outside try a cross crawl. The cross crawl is a whole body energizer, like jumping jacks, only healthier.

Stand. Begin walking in place, raising each knee as much as is comfortable. Now begin reaching down to touch your knee with the opposite hand. Touch your right hand to your left knee. Then your left hand to meet your right knee. If you are in physical shape to do so, touch your knees with your elbows as a more strenuous variation of this exercise.

Do a cross crawl for several minutes—as many as you like— to provide a quick full-body energizer that can take away drowsy feelings better than the cup of coffee you may have thought you needed. As with any exercise, the fun and benefit you experience will increase with each day.

Plan for an exercise break

Think of one time during your day that you could do leg strengthening exercises while you are standing for an extended period of time?

_____

When during your work day could you make time for a few minutes of vigorous exercise?

_____

What is one time during the day that you could do some full-body stretching exercises? Would it be possible before you get out of bed in the morning? During a break at work?

_____

What exercise could you do with your child? Would the two of you enjoy a vigorous walk together or a sport, such as tennis, if your child is older?

_____

How could you present this activity in a way that would make your child want to join you?

_____

_____

Share the stress of parenting

Parenting is best carried out as a shared activity. Parents need support and they need a break once in a while. If you are a single parent, however, finding people to share the activity may involve reaching outside your home. Wherever you need to go to find it, people support is essential to get you through difficult times.

Are there others with whom you can do cooperative childcare? Anyone you regularly see with children may be a possibility. After spending enough time together to feel comfortable leaving your child in this person's care, you can begin to exchange brief periods of respite for each of you.

Most communities have parent support groups. These groups are valuable resources for the parent who has no one else with whom to share the joys and struggles of parenting. Information is usually available through schools, social services or community colleges.

Consider taking a parenting class, if only to meet with other parents and have the opportunity to share and discuss concerns, questions, and issues regarding children the age of yours.

Even people you see casually at work or while shopping can become a valuable source of suggestions if they have time and you sincerely seek advice. People are often flattered that you would ask and are usually helpful if you ask for specific information rather than boring them with details or complaints. Asking any older person how they used to handle a parenting situation will usually result in a number of ideas, some of which may be useful.

Quietly accepting any suggestions they offer without playing "yes, but I tried that" works best. You will find out quickly whose ideas you value and who to thank for the effort and not bother to ask again.

Look for support

Do you know any parents who might like to participate in cooperative childcare? If not, where might you look for those people?

_____

_____

What support groups and classes are available in your community?

_____

_____

To whom can you go to for parenting suggestions? Make a list of people you believe to be good parents, or who might have worthwhile suggestions for you.

_____

_____

If you could ask one specific question of them, what would that be?

_____

_____

Asking for suggestions helps you to feel that others support your effort to be a good parent. And the person you ask will feel flattered that you are interested in their advice.

Though there are innumerable stresses in parenting, there are fortunately an equally wide variety of ways to confront the stress.

Be realistic about your expectations

For some parents, it is difficult to reconcile the ideal child they imagined with their actual child.

That each child is an individual goes without saying. But even your expectations of reasonable behavior must adjust to the characteristics of your unique child.

If you have only one child, spending time watching other children of the same age is the best way to get a picture of how your child is similar or different. At a neighbor's home or in a child-care center or in your child's classroom, watch other children and consider how your child may differ in energy level, attention span, interests, response to adults, and social skills.

By watching other children and by reading books that describe the general characteristics of children of this age, you can make sure that your expectations are age-appropriate. Without this comparison, many parents have unrealistic expectations of their children that frustrate everyone.

If your child is disabled, forming reasonable expectations of behavior can be even more difficult. In most communities there are associations for parents of handicapped children. They can provide you with the contacts and information you need to form expectations that are reasonable for children whose circumstances are different than those of typical children.

Whether your child differs in temperament or in abilities, it can be helpful for you to spend time around as many other children of your child's age as possible. In this way you can ensure that unreasonable expectations are not cause for additional stress upon both you and your child.

Observe other children closely

The next time you are around children the same age as your child, consider the following questions:

Are the behaviors that I struggle with in my child typical of this age? In other words, am I dealing with the same issues other parents are dealing with?

In what ways is my child different in temperament than other children? Does she seem more energetic, independent, clinging,, aggressive, shy, angry, obstinate, withdrawn, loud, or affectionate than other children in the group?

If you question whether the differences you are seeing are normal variations in temperament or indicators of specific difficulties, talk with other parents or child care providers who have more experience than you. Then, if you have additional concerns, follow up by requesting a referral to a diagnostic program through your local school district.

Comparing your child's behavior to the behavior of other children of similar age gives you the information you need to keep your expecatations reasonable and to not burden yourself by thinking your child is troubled when he is, in fact, only typical.

Develop reasonable expectations of your child

Do you believe that your child's behavior is not typical for his age?

_____

What characteristics cause you to believe this?

_____

_____

_____

Where could you go to see your child along with other children of a similar age?

_____

_____

Where in your community could you get counseling for your child if it seems necessary?

_____

_____

Accept your limitations

Much of the stress experienced in parenting is a reflection of what you expect of yourself, your desire to be an excellent parent along with your judgment as to whether you are doing a good job or a poor job in the parenting role.

Unfortunately, there is no good measure of this. It may seem that a well-behaved child reflects on your parenting skill, but this is not always true. Some children are simply more difficult than others, more demanding of time and skills.

Be realistic about what you can expect of yourself and your child

To keep your expectations of yourself reasonable, here are a few thoughts that you may find helpful.

Accept that you won't be loved 100 percent of the time. Being a parent requires you to do unpopular things: require seat belts be worn, teeth to be brushed, and homework to be completed. You have a 24-hour-a-day job, but you won't be loved and appreciated 24 hours a day.

Accept that even well-reasoned explanations and numerous expressions of your love will not necessarily make children stop wanting what they want. Give yourself permission to say "no"; give your child permission to be disappointed. It is often a parent's job to say "no" and face the child's anger.

Accept that no solution is going to last forever. Any approach to discipline may be effective for a time, and then something new will be needed. No single formula or technique will always work. And every year will be different.

Finally, accept that acquiring new parenting skills takes time, years sometimes. But even a little improvement will be welcomed by both you and your child.

Healthy parenting requires reasonable expectations of your child, yourself and the job of being a parent. There has never been a single best way to parent, nor will there ever be. The most you can expect of yourself is that yu continue to learn.

Develop healthy expectations of yourself

If you have times when you, like most parents, are disappointed in yourself as a parent, make a list of the expectations you have of yourself. Write them as completions to the sentence, "I expect myself to be." Do this quickly.

As a parent to, I expect myself be:

_____

As a parent to, I expect myself be:

_____

As a parent to, I expect myself be:

_____

As a parent to, I expect myself be:

_____

As a parent to, I expect myself be:

_____

_____

Later, after you have completed this list, show it to someone whose opinion you trust and ask how realistic it sounds.

After your conversation, put a mark next to the one, or at the most two, expectations you would most like to focus on this year. Make sure that each expectation is reasonable andis one that you could achieve if you made it a priority. Then write down the first steps you could take in the next week to begin to live up to this expectation of yourself.

If after six months you feel no progress has been made, accept that it may not be a reasonable expectation of yourself at this time. Take out your list and focus on another for the remainder of the year.